ULSTER WOMEN

A Short History, 1840–1940

Michael Sheane

ARTHUR H. STOCKWELL LTD
Torrs Park   Ilfracombe   Devon
Established 1898
www.ahstockwell.co.uk

*British Library Cataloguing-in-Publication Data.
A catalogue record for this book is available
from the British Library.*

Arthur H. Stockwell Ltd bears no responsibility
for the accuracy of information recorded in this book.

By the same author:
*Ulster & Its Future After the Troubles (1977)
Ulster & The German Solution (1978)
Ulster & The British Connection (1979)
Ulster & The Lords of the North (1980)
Ulster & The Middle Ages (1982)
Ulster & St Patrick (1984)
The Twilight Pagans (1990)
Enemy of England (1991)
The Great Siege (2002)
Ulster in the Age of Saint Comgall of Bangor (2004)
Ulster Blood (2005)
King William's Victory (2006)
Ulster Stock (2007)
Famine in the Land of Ulster (2008)
Pre-Christian Ulster (2009)
The Glens of Antrim (2010)*

ISBN 978-0-7223-4034-9
*Printed in Great Britain by
Arthur H. Stockwell Ltd
Torrs Park   Ilfracombe
Devon*

CENTRAL LIBRARY

Chapter 1

Cottage Industries

The production of goods at home was an essential part of the linen and cotton industry from the 1830s to the early 1900s. Despite industrialisation, homework remained an essential source of employment for women and an important part of the economy of the province of Ulster. In 1911, the committees of inquiry into the linen and cotton trades in Northern Ireland concluded that homework was a major part of the industrial make-up of Ulster. However, this important area of work has been mostly neglected and marginalised by historians. The tendency has been to regard homework as part-time work, which was fitted in around women's other chores. The wages were low and irregular, and were often regarded as a supplement to their husbands' pay. There is, however, a lot of evidence to show that this is a misleading and one-sided view of the work of homeworkers.

The terms *homework* and *outwork* are sometimes confused and used interchangeably by historians, but they mean two different things.

Homework, as the name implies, was generally piecework carried out in the home. The materials were distributed either directly by management from the factory or workshop, or indirectly through a series of agents throughout the country districts. In the countryside the chief method of distribution was through agents, who were usually owners of small shops.

The shirt industry, based at Londonderry, also used outstations. These were centres specially set up through the different districts. Certain days were set aside each week for the distribution and collection of materials and completed goods.

After the finished goods were returned and examined, the worker was paid in coin or in goods of the same value. All work was paid by the piece, and deductions were made from wages if there were any flaws, stains or late deliveries. Agents received 10 per cent commission on all goods completed and returned to the manufacturer. The piece rate of all work was set by the manufacturer and not by the agent.

One of the few exceptions to this was in the knitting industry, which was situated in West Donegal. Here the yarn was obtained from the mill by merchants and given out to workers in their homes. The merchants/shopkeepers made their profit from the difference between what they had been paid for the yarn and the payment received from the wholesaler for the finished articles.

Outwork was the process whereby a subcontractor – a middleman – took the work out at a given rate from the manufacturer or clothier. The middleman employed workers, often his own family, in his home or a small workshop, to do the work. The middleman could sublet part or all of the work to other subcontractors. Many worked in small factories, in regulated and unregulated workshops, and in their homes. Unlike homework, piece rates were generally set by the middleman (not by the manufacturer). Outwork was associated with the ready-to-wear industries in Great Britain and Ireland – for example, the boot-and-shoe trade, tailoring and dressmaking.

The evidence suggests that outwork was much less extensive in Ireland than on the mainland. It appears that the bulk of the work farmed out by employers in Ulster was in the form of homework.

Homework embraced a wide variety of industries – dressmaking, glovemaking, lace, knitting and others. Despite the multiplicity of occupations, most homework was based on what can be termed the sewing trades. Sewing was regarded as women's work, so the labour force was mostly female. Before 1850 work in the ready-to-wear trades and the making-up industry was done by hand. After the invention of the sewing machine in the 1850s the industry experienced some degree of modernisation and centralisation of production.

The mechanisation of industry took place in different industries at different times: in dressmaking and millinery, and in nearly all finishing processes in the tailoring and shirt trades, most work continued to be done by hand until the early 1900s; in the linen and cotton trade there was still a large amount of handwork – for example scalloping, clipping, thread-drawing, embroidery, sprigging and vice-folding. Many of the smaller industries lent themselves to handwork – for example, the lace industry. The most famous of all the centres was at Carrickmacross, where the work was carried out by hand.

The sewing machine made a great impact. In the 1860s and 1870s large stitching factories and warehouses were established in centres like Belfast, Lurgan and Londonderry. Between 1855 and 1878 the shirt industry brought employment to Londonderry. By 1871, 2,229 operatives were employed in sixteen concerns, with another twenty smaller factories employing between fifty and 100 persons each.

The belief that large numbers would be drawn into factories proved to be false. Both the employers and the workers were quick to realise the versatility of the sewing machine for use in the home. Hand and treadle machines were introduced for homeworkers in great numbers from the 1860s onwards. The shirt manufacturers at Londonderry hired out new and second-hand machines without charge on condition that a given number of articles were made each week. Most machines were expensive. They were bought under easy-term agreements or were hired for about 1s. to 1s. 6d. per week. Between 1874 and 1900 over 3,000 Singer sewing machines were sold in the Londonderry area.

Homework survived, and it expanded chiefly because it produced considerable cost savings to the manufacturer. Under industrialisation the production process was subdivided into small tasks, with each worker assigned to a single operation. Most tasks were quickly learned, requiring little or no supervision; they could be performed by women, children and the elderly. The already existing pool of surplus female labour enabled manufacturers to keep labour costs to a minimum. Wages paid for work at home were lower than those paid in the factory, even if the same work was being done. As well as this, the employer made savings on capital investment in buildings and machinery, supervision, training, heating, lighting and other overhead costs.

Homeworkers were also without the protection of the Factory and Workshop Acts. A home labour force enabled manufacturers to avoid restrictive legislation on hours and health. This flexibility was of the greatest importance for the manufacturer – particularly in the linen industry, where orders for the United States were increasing. In order to help the dispatch of these orders, homeworkers had to work from early in the morning until late at night. Homework was suited to the cyclical peaks and troughs of the linen industry, and the seasonal nature of trades such as dressmaking and tailoring. Work in the home could be easily expanded at times of great demand, at little or no cost to the employer other than wages; during recessions they could be dispensed with without any great loss to the employer. All this made homework very attractive to employers.

It is not surprising that the ratio of homeworkers to factory workers ranged between three to one and four to one. In 1863, for example, in Londonderry in the shirt-and-collar industry, Robert Sinclair employed 500 factory workers to 2,000 outside workers. At Welsh, Margetson & Co., the proportion was roughly 200 factory workers to 900 homeworkers. This remained constant until the 1900s. In 1889 the Inspector of Factories was able to report that one company in Londonderry was employing 1,200 inside and 3,000 outside workers. Two other firms, employing about 600 factory workers each, were giving work to 1,500 and 2,000 respectively through their stations.

In many homes it was the practice for one person to register with an employer, but the work was carried out by two, three or more members of the family. The number of homeworkers was therefore greater than quoted above.

The low ratio of factory workers to homeworkers was not unique to Ireland. In the early 1890s, a Miss Collet said that in Bristol three-quarters of the work was done in homes, with the ratio between homeworkers and factory workers being about five to one. In some firms the ratio was sometimes as great as twelve to one.

The two systems, homework and factory work, were neither separate nor competing, but together they formed a complete system. For example, in the making of handkerchiefs work was often handed out late in the afternoon or after the factory had closed. The work generally had to be ready for the following morning, often before the factory opened, so that the factory workers could complete the next stage. The handkerchiefs were then ready to be sent out to homeworkers to be embroidered before the final stage of production. There was considerable pressure on all workers to work quickly.

Many historians have regarded homework in the clothing or other industries as uneconomic or wasteful, but contemporaries had a very different perspective. Many owners believed that they could compete effectively with home and foreign competitors by employing home labour. In 1907 a Miss Martindale described the increase in demand for imported goods, such as tablecloths, ladies' underwear, napkins and handkerchiefs. The demand was met by increasing the volume of work to homeworkers. A large surplus labour force meant that the total number of homeworkers could be varied with demand, and this, combined with large savings on capital expenditure, ensured that the manufacturers retained a firm commitment to the farming-out of work.

Homework was a very large industry, with its own occupational subdivisions. The embroidery and sprigging industries were centred on Belfast, but homework also provided work for women in counties Antrim, Down, Donegal, Fermanagh and Tyrone. Sprigging was white embroidery – the working of a pattern with a needle on white cloth. The industry had its origin in the stitched-muslin trade established at Donaghadee in 1829. Agents were appointed for the large Glasgow houses, and the trade rapidly expanded into the Ulster counties. In 1849 the muslin industry was said to be employing a total of nearly 180,000 persons and spending £400,000 annually on wages. By the 1850s this had reached £1,400,000. The muslin industry collapsed in the 1860s and early 1870s, but the embroidery business re-emerged in the 1880s and 1890s, when there was a great demand for embroidered linen and cotton goods. By the early 1990s the industry was estimated to be still spending £250,000 on wages.

The shirt industry came to Londonderry in the 1840s, and by the 1860s it had expanded into counties Londonderry, Donegal and Tyrone. The industry was most important in counties Londonderry and Donegal. By 1901 shirt-makers and seamstresses accounted for 40.2 per cent and 34.8 per cent respectively of the total number of females in employment. In County Donegal the greatest concentration of shirt-makers was along the Inishowen Peninsula, where one-quarter of those recorded in the census lived. By 1890 the shirt industry had a turnover of over £1 million. A decade later the trade was still spending over £200,000 annually on wages.

The town of Lurgan in County Armagh was the centre of the handkerchief business. After Belfast, it was said to be the most important town in the province. The handkerchief business provided employment for thousands of women in the districts of Lurgan, Portadown, Dromore and Bambridge. In 1887, Mr Woodgate, a factory inspector, said that every female, married or not, was supplied with ample means of work in the thread-drawing, veining, hemstitching and folding industries.

The town of Glenties and nearby neighbourhoods – for example, Bambridge in County Donegal – were the chief centres for the machine and hand-knitting industries. The knitting industry was one of the poorest paid, but it provided essential work in those districts noted for extreme poverty.

The homespun-tweed industry was for the most part based in counties Mayo and Kerry, and South-West Donegal in the districts of Carrick and Ardara. As in the linen trade, homespun provided employment for an entire family, the wool being carded, dyed, spun and woven by the household.

In the 1890s the quality of homespun was improved with the help of the Congested District Board and the Irish Industrial Council, but there was little development of the trade in the 1900s. Wages remained low, women earning about 7d. for two days' work carding and spinning. In 1897–8 only about £5,000 was spent on wages for the industry in Ardara and Carrick. In the early 1900s it was estimated that about 1,000 females were involved in the homespun industry around Carrick and Ardara.

The lace industry dated from about the time of the Great Famine. Under the influence of women philanthropists, an occupation previously earmarked for 'ladies' was transformed into employment for the peasantry. At the beginning of the twentieth century the lace industry underwent a revival under the influence of the Irish Lace Depot, the Irish Industrial School and the Congested District Board. Lace was partly produced in the homes of the workers, and there was work in lace production in counties Sligo, Donegal and Down. The largest part of the industry, however, was concentrated in counties Armagh, Fermanagh and Monaghan.

It is impossible to ascertain the size of the home workforce, despite attempts to do so under the Factory and Workshop Act (1901). Employers were obliged to send lists of outworkers and homeworkers twice yearly to the local councils. The reason for this was to ensure that the premises of the workers were available for inspection by the parish health officers. However, this section of the Act was not applied to the making-up of clothes until 1911.

The legislation proved to be inadequate. Only a few of the larger towns, like Belfast, Lurgan and Londonderry, made any attempt to comply with it. Even so, the returns represented only a fraction of the total number employed. In Lurgan, where thousands were employed, returns of 1,400 employees were made. The act was ignored to such an extent that when the commissioners for the 1911 Linen Inquiry sent circulars to all the local district councils in Ulster almost none replied. The best the commissioners could report was that the homeworkers probably outnumbered the 22,000 employed in factories and workshops in the linen making-up trade, but this estimate was based on inadequate information.

There is evidence to show that the work was not carried out with any enthusiasm in the home. Many women did not report themselves as employed to the enumerators, the reason being partly that they did not regard their work as 'real' work and partly because of fear of officialdom. Where other sources are used to supplement the census figures it is clear that there was a gross under-numeration of women employed in their homes.

It is impossible to ascertain the number of women working in the home, but contemporary records, especially those of the lady inspectors, enable us to see the extent of work that was carried on in certain rural areas. It appears that wherever homework was established it generally expanded rapidly to employ thousands in the surrounding districts. For example, Donegal, despite its isolation, was a major employer of homeworkers in the last quarter of the nineteenth century. Miss Martindale reported the proliferation of agents over large parts of County Donegal, especially in the embroidery and sprigging industries in the southern part of the county.

Agents usually worked for several different firms, and each agent was responsible for providing work for several hundred people. In Ballintrae one agent had 600 people on his books, and another in County Donegal had 700. A sprigging agent in Donegal paid £1,000 in wages in six months for one Glasgow firm alone. In Ardara, two tweed merchants employed many women for embroidery and knitting. Women who registered for work usually collected work for others in the family, so increasing the number of homeworkers still further. According to the women inspectors, agents were dotted all over the smaller regions. For example, at Killybegs there were seven agents and another two close by. Mr McNeill, secretary to the Glenties Poor Law Union, calculated that 75 per cent of the property of the union was valued under £4 per year. Poverty was rife in the extreme, and men and women were forced to supplement their incomes by whatever means were available. McNeill estimated that there were about 180 agents employing about 12,000 families, four or five to a family, in sprigging, knitting and thread-drawing.

Not all of the women worked all year round, but many, especially at times of trade booms, were able to obtain work at some time of the year. Their labour should have been recorded in the census. Contemporary investigations show the great gap between the economic reality and the results of the census. For example, the numbers of women recorded under the main category of Textiles and Fabrics in the 1901 census for County Donegal were: embroidery, 903; woollen manufacture, 565; and fancy goods, 1,626. This was a gross underestimate.

A main aspect of homework, from its inception and throughout the period, was that it was not confined to working-class women. In towns throughout the province homeworkers were described as widows and spinsters, or married women whose husbands had low wages or who were out of work. A large number of women were forced to work to feed themselves. However, there were also women that were better off – the wives of artisans and other skilled workers whose husbands earned good wages. This group of women was referred to by Clementina Black as Class D or 'reprehensible' women. They were able to live off their husbands' wages, but they preferred to engage in paid work. The Class D women earned what was described as 'pin money' or 'pocket money'.

In the country districts homeworkers were mainly the wives and daughters of smallholders, farmers and agricultural labourers. The economic class of rural homeworkers ranged from very poor labourers to well-off tenant farmers. Some of the tenant farmers were described by Miss Collet as typically Irish, but very well off. The home labour force was not confined to lower-class women. Some homeworkers lived in respectable conditions, the rental of their houses ranging from 2s. 6d. and 3s. 6d. for working-class houses to as much as £30 per year. This social and economic diversity was largely due to the perception of homework as a respectable occupation. Firstly, sewing and embroidery was a woman's occupation, a genteel art learned from childhood; secondly, work was carried out in the home, so it was possible to disguise the number of hours spent each week on paid work. Homework could be portrayed as something secondary to a woman's role as a housewife and mother. Respectable upper- and middle-class women were expected to fulfil their role as housewives and mothers and to be dependent upon their husbands, but homework was considered respectable for these women.

The hourly rates were low, and the work was erratic. Many of the women were on or below the poverty line, despite working long hours. Wages of 3s. 6d. per week were earned in most homework trades, including thread-drawing, clipping, folding, scalloping and embroidery. Even enthusiastic workers employed in relatively well-paid sewing-machine work could only expect to earn a net wage of 8s. to 9s. per week. Women living on their own, or with a family to support, suffered the worst extremes of poverty. Long hours and low standards of living were found to be the norm in a government inquiry into the linen and making-up trades.

A Mrs S. had laboured as a thread-drawer in Lurgan for fifteen years. She was married to a weaver and had several children. The eldest was thirteen. Her husband left for work at six o'clock. After preparing breakfast she began work at eight o'clock and worked constantly through the day until ten or eleven o'clock at night. If there was an urgent order that had to be completed for the next morning she had to stay and complete it no matter what the hour. The eldest child worked with her mother until about seven o'clock at night. The only breaks Mrs S. took were to prepare dinner and tea for the family, which took about two hours for dinner and one hour for tea. Mrs S. earned 12s. per week, and the combined wage of mother and child averaged 6s. to 7s. 6d. per week. All of the husband's wages and that of the child were handed over to Mrs S., who took charge of the family budgeting. She stated that the total weekly income of 18s. to 19s. was mostly spent on food and rent. There was nothing left for extras.

Mrs H. performed the heavy work of clipping thread from large valances and sheets. Her two eldest boys, aged nine and eleven, worked alongside her. The boys were generally awakened at about six o'clock so that she could get three dozen completed before breakfast at eight o'clock. She stopped work to prepare breakfast for her husband, and started to work again almost immediately afterwards, continuing until eleven or twelve at night. The boy of nine generally laboured until seven o'clock at night, but when the situation demanded he was compelled to work until one o'clock in the morning. In common with other women, Mrs H.'s only break in the day was for the preparation of food. This work had to be carried out on a daily basis. Large and heavy parcels had to be returned to the factory and carried up six flights of narrow stairs, but Mrs H. was not in good health and was unable to carry them herself; the task was always done by her young sons. Mrs H. and her two children earned about 6s. per week, and her husband earned between £1 and 30s. per week. For a working-class man in Ireland this was a reasonable wage, but the labour of the mother and her children was believed to be essential to sustain the family. Many wives economically worse off than Mrs H. worked long, uninterrupted hours on a regular basis throughout the year. Widows and deserted wives seem to have been amongst the homeworkers in the worst plight. Such women were often either the sole support of their families or the chief breadwinners. Women with husbands who had been out of work for some considerable time, perhaps owing to poor health, were sometimes even worse off. They had the task of supporting themselves, their husbands and their children, and sometimes they also had to pay expensive medical bills.

For example, Mrs J.'s husband had been unable to work for a long time because of bad health. She had five children, the eldest of whom was a daughter aged ten. She had no choice but to withdraw her daughter from school so that she could assist with clipping and scalloping. The girl worked from the small hours of the morning until late at night – sometimes until two o'clock in the morning. As well as this, the daughter had to look after Mrs J.'s other young children. The only break in labour was if there was a shortage of work. The mother said that she was unable to allow her daughter any playtime. The only break available was a short walk for some fresh air on Sundays. The most Mrs J. could earn was 5s. 3d. per week.

The entire family was supported on these small earnings. Apart from occasional help from charity, she had to support two adults and five children on a maximum of 9d. per head per week.

Mrs C., a widow, collected 6d. worth of work in the morning and constantly made handkerchiefs. During their school dinner break, her children clipped what she had sewn, and then she continued working until about four o'clock, when the children came home from school. The children brought home another 4d. or 6d. worth of work, which she would have to complete that night. During February 1911 her weekly earnings were 4s. 9d., 2s. 8d., 3s. 5d. and 3s. 7d. As well as this she had 3s. 6d. assistance from charity.

Despite her obvious poverty, Mrs C. was more lucky than many others. According to Miss Galway in Belfast, some aged homeworkers and young widows found that it was impossible to support themselves without help. Only a small number of those in need actually received any help from friendly societies and charities. Without additional assistance some women and their families had to make do with less food when there was no work, and sometimes they were unable to buy any food at all. There is no way of knowing how numerous this section of the homeworkers was.

In 1897 a survey by the Women's Industrial Council revealed that over 40 per cent of homeworkers were the sole breadwinners. According to Booth's survey in 1901, 20 per cent of dressmakers, shirt-makers and seamstresses were heads of households. Clementina Black found that 28.4 per cent of women workers supported a family, and 64.5 per cent of them worked because of their husbands' poor wages.

The women who suffered most were deserted wives, widows, spinsters, and wives with husbands on very low and irregular wages. The poverty of the poorest section of the homeworkers was worsened by the erratic nature of wages. Most homeworkers experienced some degree of fluctuation in their pay. Wages were reduced when women had to work on poorer-paid articles or when there was a shortage of work.

Mrs Y., for example, received 9d. per dozen for sewing coloured pinafores and aprons, but on the coarser white work she only received 5d. per dozen. The drop in wages was sometimes only slight, but for the poorest women a drop of 1s. would have been a substantial decrease. Any reduction of income for women on or below the subsistence level, even for a short time, was potentially very serious. If sufficient money was not earned to cover the cost of food and rent, many homeworkers survived by extending their debts with their agents or shopkeepers. In many areas throughout the province it was common for agents who were also shopkeepers to pay women in goods from their shops. When the price of goods bought by homeworkers exceeded their wages they could either pay the difference or arrange to have the goods on credit.

Although credit was often vital for the survival of families, the debt became an added burden: extra hours had to be worked so that the debt could be paid off. The longer the drop in wages, the greater the need to work longer, uninterrupted hours. In many cases women struggling to repay their debts found themselves at the mercy of the agents. An agent could induce workers to take work that was poorly paid since they were in his debt; even though there was an abundance of work, women could not necessarily choose the best-paid jobs. Poorer people were forced to spend as much time as possible on their paid work, leaving only a minimum of time for cooking, cleaning and childcare. A working day of fourteen to sixteen hours six days per week was common. Those that earned the least per hour were driven to work more and more hours. Poverty meant that they had to rush the housework so that they could spend an extra few minutes at their trade, earning an extra few farthings. Normally about two or three hours per day was spent on cooking and cleaning, but in some cases women who did not have husbands to prepare lunch for chose to work on rather than take even a short lunch break. The heavier tasks of scrubbing and washing were, for the most part, performed on Saturday afternoons. However, a lot of women could not afford to take this time at weekends for housework. Time spent on sewing, for example, could not be devoted to household duties. Women without children had to collect and return the work themselves. Even when the women lived close to the factory workshop, this could take an hour every day. In rural districts, Miss Squires found that it was not uncommon for women to walk as much as eighteen miles to their agent.

For the poorest workers, a day off work was not possible. Many women continued to work at sewing and embroidery when they had sore eyes and failing sight. Sometimes they continued even though they realised that the work had not only affected their health but would continue to aggravate it.

Mrs L. was lucky in that her sight was not badly affected, and she was able to find work as a charwoman, but she had to support her children and an ill husband. Her health had started to deteriorate, but she was not able to reduce her heavy workload. Her case is typical of the thousands of women who suffered ill health and were not able to fall back upon charity. Generally poor physical health meant that more hours had to be worked to compensate for the reduced rate of output. Only when their children grew up could these women relax.

These homeworkers worked out of financial need, and their earnings, though small, were essential to obtain the basic necessities of food and shelter. The pressures of work prevented a domestic ideology from dominating their daily lives in the same way as that of the middle classes. Despite this, it appears that they derived at least part of their identity from their domestic duties, and they expressed pride in their domestic role. They expressed the fact that the family could not survive without their work. If the work was hard on them and their children, they had no choice but to keep working; otherwise the family would become destitute. Women would have seen this as a failure in their domestic role as wives and mothers.

Mrs J., for example, who worked with her children seven days per week, was proud that her work kept the family from being maintained by charity. As she was receiving assistance for the rent she wished to prove that she was doing what she could.

For married homeworkers, status was obtained from working. In keeping with middle-class beliefs, pride and being a good wife and mother were interrelated.

A small section of the homeworkers was drawn from the ranks of a higher social class – women who were not motivated by the same financial necessity as their poorer counterparts. It was claimed that women in Class D generally laboured to add to their comforts: to obtain a higher standard of living and have money which they could save or spend as they wished. Because they did not work out of financial necessity, some historians have assumed that their work experience and their conception of their economic role was distinctly different. They seem to have worked fewer hours in the day, but on a much more irregular basis. This draws a picture of women working at a more leisurely pace, stopping and starting their work in a casual manner. Cohen suggests that their paid work was done when it could be fitted around the housework. Closely connected to this argument is the opinion that these women derived their identity from their domestic role. Paid work was secondary to the progress of their existence.

It is fraught with difficulty to ascertain the extent to which women divided their time between paid work and housework. Not all the responses from women were as detailed as those given in the 1911 Linen Inquiry. The middle-class investigators assumed that women would be able to state clearly the number of hours that they spent on paid work and the number of hours they set aside for housework and leisure. The responses from the women were not very clear as to the division of their day.

Miss Collet complained about the extent to which women sat around not too keen to work.

Women generally started the paid work at about nine o'clock in the morning. Like their poorer counterparts, they continued to work until about ten o'clock at night. It appears that some of the women took time off during the day to cook and clean and for meals. It is, however, necessary to stress that these breaks were not long – an estimate of five or six hours out of a fourteen- or fifteen-hour working day. Work was a central factor, and there is some evidence that work for the most part was carried out regularly throughout the year. Whenever these women were employed they had to work long hours. One of the most obvious reasons for this was because of the low pay rates of 1d. to 2d. per hour. Even these low rates were only possible if work was carried out regularly, and at a fast pace. Investigators found that in most cases where women's wages were low it was not the result of intermittent and casual labour by the women, but because of the low piece rates, lack of work or disability. Secondly, it was the standard practice, irrespective of the industry, for the distributor to set a time and date for the completion of the work. In country districts work was collected once or twice a week. In towns work was often collected on a daily basis and had to be returned early the next morning. Homework and factory work were closely related, and late deliveries from the cottage producers often meant that workers in the factory would be slack or idle.

Rushed orders were common throughout the linen industry and cotton trades, and this resulted in additional pressures on women and agents to meet deadlines. The number of rushed orders varied. They could be handed out two or three times per week, or there might be none at all for three months. The pressures on these people are clear. It was reported that the towns and villages were filled with women who sat up late into the night in order to meet deadlines for exports for the United States. Agents who could command the greatest number of women prepared to work into the night had the best chance of securing large orders from the factories. They received 10 per cent commission, and it was in their best interest to employ reliable women. Women who gave housework priority over their homework would not be considered for regular work, and in many cases they were taken off the books altogether. One agent said that for ten years he had carried out a policy of ending the employment for women whom he considered were bad workers. Nevertheless, homeworkers were often in demand and there were opportunities for women to take small amounts of work and earn a pittance per day. Others worked only when their husbands' income was reduced. The evidence shows that homeworkers of this type comprised only a small minority of homeworkers.

The poorest women were motivated to work by financial necessity; the better-off homeworkers could have also had financial pressures. *Necessity* is a relative term. For some women it was essential to work to maintain outward respectability which would distinguish them from the lower social groups. There was a wide variety of subdivisions within the working class, each with its own ideas of status. For many working females it was necessary to have a better standard of dress and housing than poorer sectors. Other women thought that more money was essential to avoid debt or to provide a good education for their children. It was absolutely paramount for people to maintain their social status. For example, one woman who lived with her widowed father worked to have money of her own and to keep the house clean beyond reproach. Women in better economic straits informed investigators that they would be prepared to give up paid work and the benefits that this brought. Some displayed a degree of shame regarding their paid work, but others were proud of their economic contribution to their homes.

The poorer classes had no alternative but to work. Women in

better economic circumstances had a choice, as they could survive with a reduced standard of living. Choosing employment was a positive response to the economic situation. Work meant that these women maintained respectability. They did not see their work role and social status as being conflicting. They saw themselves as good mothers since they were able to work and provide a good standard of living for themselves and their family. These women stressed the fact that their decision to work meant that their families were better off.

Homework was of the greatest importance because it demonstrated the acceptance of work beyond the narrow confines of the lower working-class people. Even amongst the skilled working classes and small tradespeople, paid work and respectability were not mutually exclusive. On the one hand, their identity was to some extent centred on their home and family, but they rejected the old idea that respectable women should not undertake paid work. Along with the lower working classes, their values were changed as a result of economic pressures.

Homework was a time-consuming and exhausting occupation, leaving little time for domestic and farm work. The fact that the home was also the workplace meant that small houses, already overcrowded, were littered with parcels or worksheets, and whatever materials were being worked upon. The larger the number of homeworkers, the greater the volume of work and the resultant litter and confusion. One of the main problems was the way in which large valances and other items were stuffed. All this had to be removed before work could begin, and floors were often covered in paper.

Thread-drawing could be done more quickly if the linen was dampened. As a result it was common for the cloth to be wet with a mixture of tallow and water, thus softening it. After the thread-drawing had been completed, the handkerchiefs, tablecloths and sheets were hung on lines in the kitchen to dry. They eventually had to be taken down, folded and parcelled for return to the agent. All this was included in the workload of the women; it also increased the untidy appearance of the houses, and reduced the living space for the family.

Two methods by which women managed their heavy workload were by employing their children and elderly members of the family. Their co-operation was often essential. It appears that the use of child labour from the ages of six and seven years of age was commonplace. Systematic investigations found that the boys and girls often worked before and after school until late into the night. In the districts of Lurgan, Portadown and Dromore the employment of mothers and children in the home was widespread. Mr McCaffrey, the district inspector for the National Schools, reported that children generally worked before and after school in Lurgan and the surrounding districts, chiefly at thread-drawing and clipping. As in other areas, children were made to miss school two or three days per week in order to work. He drew a picture of women and children crowded around a table in the middle of their small kitchen drawing threads and hemstitching until late into the night. Until about the age of thirteen, homework was often performed by both sexes. The need to earn the next few pence overrode any notions of what was boys' work or girls' work, and children assisted in whatever way they could. If they could not sew, embroider or knit, they could still be used for other tasks. They could carry work from the distribution centre or clip and fold it to be ready to be sewn on machines, as well as other tasks.

Mrs C.'s children could sometimes add two or three shillings to her week's pay. They often worked long hours to earn an extra few pence.

Sewing-machine work had many preparatory stages, such as the folding of straps and tucking-in of corners. Children carried out the work continuously at the sewing machine and increased their family's total earnings. Children's earnings were incorporated into the wages of their mothers or older sisters. It is impossible in many cases to estimate the value of their work. Children's labour points to the existence of a family-based system of work and a collective wage. One of the most obvious factors in Ulster homework was the extent to which adult women co-operated over the preparation of goods, and the very small numbers of women who worked alone.

Inspectors visited approximately 1,700 homes in London, the provinces and Northern Ireland for the 1907 Select Committee on Homework. Out of 737 homes visited in rural areas and small urban districts through counties Down, Londonderry, Tyrone and East Donegal, only 20 per cent of women were found to be working alone. This figure would have been even lower if the labour of children had been taken into account.

It was common for two, three and sometimes more members of a family to be homeworkers. The women normally co-operated closely with each other in regard to paid and unpaid labour. The evidence suggests that mothers and daughters, grandmothers, aunts and nieces formed a sort of combined unit. The common practice was for one member of the family to register with an agent and collect and return the work for many members of the household, who performed the same or different tasks at different rates of pay.

Within this system of pay it was possible for each member to estimate their own particular outputs and earnings. The lady inspectors discovered that in households where several members worked, little or no attempt was made to estimate how much each person earned. In most cases they found it very difficult to obtain a rough idea of individual weekly earnings. The problem was so widespread that the inspectors were forced to base their estimates on the earnings of women who worked alone. There were wage differences in households, because some women might be working on higher-paid work and some were capable of greater output than others. The fact that so many women made little or no attempt to ascertain their individual pay may point to the fact that wage differences between members were not seen as a problem. Distinctions were not made between the wages of each person because the important issue was the family's total pay.

Homework differed according to the many levels of ability of family members. The old, the disabled, and those with poor eyesight and other forms of bad health could not produce work at the same rate as those that were in good health. By being flexible a family was able to maximise output, and homework lent itself well to this approach. Many tasks were simple – easily learnt for the young and elderly – and they could be divided up to suit the workers. For example, children and the elderly or physically disabled could work in accordance with their abilities, undertaking clipping, thread-drawing and preparatory handwork for the sewing machines.

Another method of increasing production was to divide a large task into smaller sections. Co-operation was particularly beneficial where women were disabled because of age or ill health.

One woman, a Miss I., lived with her niece, and both women worked at lace-clipping and top-sewing from nine o'clock in the morning until eleven at night. The niece had shaper eyesight, so she performed all the finer work, while her aunt did the coarser work. The niece, however, was not too strong, so her aunt carried the work to and from the distributor. In periods of recession they could earn 5s. or 6s. between them, but when work was plentiful the niece was able to earn more than her aunt. They pooled their wages and the aunt's pension and shared the burden of food and rent. On her own the niece would have had great difficulty obtaining work, and the inability of the aunt to perform fine work would have reduced her income.

The main target was to earn as much as possible to maintain an acceptable standard of living. Widows and single women benefited much from living with female relatives or sharing the costs of rent, food and heating, since a subsistence wage was paid to most homeworkers.

The same flexible approach to labour is evident in regard to the allocation of household and farm tasks. On smaller farms the women still carried out many tasks, including the care of poultry and pigs, milking and dairy work, planting and lifting potatoes, cutting and carrying turf and assisting during harvests. In some families women devoted themselves entirely to sewing and embroidery; in others, women were employed mainly on farm and household duties. The priority of the tasks varied in accordance with the needs of the household. At peak periods more time was allocated to field labour. In regions such as the Rosses and Glenties the majority of the men worked as migratory labourers, leaving the women to work on the small family holdings. Agents expected a drop in the homework output of women during the summer months when their help was needed on the land.

It was reported that some women in urban areas tended to concentrate on homework throughout the day, while others worked mainly on the cooking and cleaning. There was sometimes an overlap of duties between the women for a given household. Those who concentrated on paid work also carried out the heavier domestic chores, like washing. Women who concentrated on the household chores often helped with the parcelling and folding aspects of homework.

The life of the homeworkers was markedly different from that of factory workers. Their working day was not marked by a clear separation between home-related tasks and paid work, and the pay was often earned collectively. The hours of the clock did not define the beginning and end of the working day. Homework had a great deal of continuity with the pre-industrial past, where work was performed in the home, mainly on a collective basis, and all members of the family contributed what they could afford to the support of the family. Homework for the most part was sweated labour, with women obliged to work for low pay. Moreover the system in Ireland tended to place women very much at the mercy of the agents. Only during trade booms, like that of the early 1900s, were women able to exercise any choice as to the type of work they performed. Homework was an important part of the infrastructure of Ulster, especially in the rural districts. It injected cash into the districts and stimulated growth. Money was, for the most part, spent within the locality, the buying of groceries and household goods stimulating the growth of small agent/shopkeepers and raising the general standard of living of the community.

Paid work was a central feature of the lives of many working-class women. The wages of the wives and children were essential for the survival of the family. We should not permit twenty-first-century conceptions of real work and a real wage to detract from the economic importance of homework industries for both women and manufacturers. Homework at times was disorganised, but it should not be excluded from studies of the labour market.

Chapter 2

The Belfast Ladies' Institute

The growth of towns and cities in Britain throughout the nineteenth century has been well recorded, as has the social progress of the times. One development was the provision of public organised education for boys and girls of the lower and middle classes. During the 1850s and 1860s there was an increasing interest in the provision of higher education for women in England and Ireland. In Ireland there were several reasons for this. The system of national education, supported by the government, had been established in Ireland since 1831. National Schools were set up all over the country, providing free elementary education for boys and girls in the remote villages. The system was mainly aimed at the lower classes.

In the nineteenth century intelligent and interested middle-class women were becoming increasingly concerned by the lack of adequate education for girls, and they were determined to seek out a remedy. On the other hand there were endowed schools for boys throughout Ireland. These schools, like the Royal Belfast Academical Institution and the Royal Schools in Armagh and Dungannon, bridged the gap between primary and university education for boys. Their sisters were not so well off for educational opportunities.

The nineteenth century was a time of rapid urbanisation. When women remained unmarried, or when a family business declined or the male head of a household died, the city-based family, including the women, had to find paid work to support themselves. Girls who had little or no formal education could not compete successfully for jobs. Even those who had attended a seminary for young girls had no proof of educational achievement for there were no public examinations. Women who had left school and had not secured a formal occupation often wanted to continue their education. Women not only wanted to occupy their time but they wanted to expand their knowledge and gain qualifications.

In these straits the Belfast Ladies' Institute was formed in 1867. Similar institutions existed on the mainland, and at Dublin and Belfast. Dublin only expanded slightly in the nineteenth century, but Belfast followed the course laid out by the cities of Manchester and Glasgow. Belfast was developing rapidly as a port, market town and commercial centre, with an expanding middle class. Belfast grew faster than any other city in the United Kingdom. The population, which was less than 20,000 in 1800, had increased to 349,000 by 1900.

Six women founded the Belfast Ladies' Institute: Mrs Bushell, Mrs McIlwaine, Mrs J. Scott Porter, Mrs Duffin, Miss Stevelly and Miss Cunningham. All came from prosperous families, and underlined the importance of a good education for women. For example, Mr Bushell was a stockbroker and a wine-and-spirits merchant. The Reverend William McIlwaine was rector of St George's, High Street, Belfast. The Reverend Dr J. Scott Porter was the minister of the Second Presbyterian Church, Belfast. Mr Duffin owned a flax-spinning mill, and Professor Stevelly was a lecturer at Queen's College, Belfast. The same class of women provided the leading figures in the institute throughout its existence. Many held the post of Lady Superintendent for some years. Mrs Duffin was still on the committee at the last meeting in 1897, but this was exceptional service; it was usual for women to hold office for a shorter time. For example, some women had to resign when their husbands left Belfast, as Professor Thomson did in July 1873. Mrs Murphy had to resign for she could not manage to attend meetings in March 1878. The members of the institute were mostly middle-class, being the wives and daughters of clergymen, insurance agents, distillers and textile manufacturers.

The Belfast Ladies' Institute's objective was to provide, for ladies, advanced classes of a higher standard than had hitherto been available in the locality. This experiment in education was meant to broaden the opportunities for women. The institute aimed to employ professors at Queen's College, Belfast and to offer a high standard of teaching. They planned to hold examinations at the end of each session to provide proof of achievement. The Belfast Ladies' Institute was well supported with elected officers and members. In an attempt to stimulate interest in the project, the Marchioness of Dufferin and Ava was chosen as president, and ladies Lurgan, Adair, Annesley and Cairns were invited to be vice presidents. Lady Dufferin accepted the presidency, and the lady overseers outlined the progress of the institute. Any lady could become a member by the payment of a minimum of five shillings.

There were originally six lady overseers, but their number rose to eight in 1870 and ten in 1871. These officials were expected to be present at all meetings of the institute. There were about seven committee meetings every six months. Committee meetings were generally held in the homes of the institute's lady overseers, like Mrs Porter's home in College Square East, Mrs Burden's in College Square North, Miss Isabel's in Claremont Street and Mrs Duffin's at Strandtown Lodge.

There was a high feminist spirit in the society, but their treasurer was always male and the organisation relied upon men to preside at the open meetings, for it was almost unheard of for women to hold such important posts. In 1870 Lord Dufferin was asked to take the chair at a meeting of the institute. Invitations were sent to the Bishop of Down, Connor and Dromore, the Mayor of Belfast, the professors at Queen's College and businessmen. The support of the Belfast community was vital to the success of the Belfast Ladies' Institute. They delivered the inaugural address of the institute in 1870 and offered to write a booklet on the higher education of women.

Suitable premises for the institute's committee meetings and its classes were hard to find in Belfast. The museum in College Square North, owned by the Belfast Natural History and Philosophical Society, was the chosen venue of the institute, and the museum is often made available free of charge. The ladies' lectures were generally held for two hours on Monday and Thursday afternoons. At one time a room in the museum was set aside for the ladies' disrobing, but it was decided that this was unnecessary and that the hall would be sufficient.

During the first session in 1867–8 five subjects were available to the 187 students. Professor Nesbitt taught English language and literature, Professor Thomson took charge of geography, the Reverend Dr J. Scott Porter talked politics and historical geography, Mr Wild took French language and literature and Dr Hodges taught economic science.

It was perhaps difficult to hold scientific classes in a building which had not been designed for this purpose. The institute's porter was given a large bonus of £1 for the trouble connected with the chemistry classes. Cookery classes were also hard to fit in. In 1873 the secretary was deputed to enquire about the use of the music hall in May Street, Belfast, but it was decided that the Manor Hall of the Ulster Hall was best suited for this purpose. In regard to art tuition, it was hoped that lectures would be held in the Government School of Art, housed in the north wing of the Royal Belfast Academical Institution. In some cases the availability of lecturers were subject to the popularity of courses. The lady overseers were eager to have a wide range of subjects, often with a scientific bent. A survey of courses over the years shows this clearly. However, the main subjects of the institute between 1867 and 1897 were English language and literature, the most popular area of women's interest, and these classes were always full. Other subjects ranged from English history to German and French language and literature, Latin and botany. It was proposed that these courses should be supplemented with lectures in astronomy, numerology, physiology, theory of music, chemistry and zoology. Not all of this materialised. In 1872 it was not possible to run classes in geometry and the theory and practice of arithmetic, even though a number of girls were interested. Local doctors, like Dr Redfern, Professor Cummings and Dr Browne, were invited to give talks on the laws of health, but the topic was not pursued.

Given the low educational standard of women in the mid-nineteenth century it is understandable that the Belfast Ladies' Institute should try to lift the intellectual aspirations of their students; but if the intention was to provide extra skills to facilitate female employment, numerology and astronomy would appear to have been of little use, except for the sake of teaching. These were not usual topics of study in the ladies' seminary. It is more likely that, in offering the subjects, the organisers wanted to challenge the common perception that young ladies could only expect to acquire the ability to sing, paint on satin or velvet and appear to advantage at a concert or ball.

The ladies had to rely on the men to teach the academic classes, for there were insufficient educated women in Belfast to undertake such classes at a high level. Most of the lecturers were professors at Queen's College or local celebrities in the sciences and arts. For example, Dr Andrews, vice president of Queen's College, taught chemistry; Dr Hodges, of the Chemical-Agricultural Society, lectured in the 1867–8 session; and Mr Nixon was obviously a man of many talents, capable of teaching both arithmetic and English. Another important teacher was Professor Wyville Thomson, an eminent zoologist. He was knighted in 1876 and was professor of mineralogy, geology and natural history. Later he was head of the Challenger Expedition, which carried out deep-sea diving explorations. He was a firm supporter of the Belfast Ladies' Institute. Another supporter was the Belfast naturalist Robert Patterson, who delivered papers on zoology to the institute from 1870 until he died in 1872.

There were also two other courses, less academic in character – cookery and art. These attracted large numbers of females. The only classes run by females were cookery classes, and these were conducted by Mrs Price, leading to a certificate in the Government School of Science and Art at Kensington Collegiate School. The certificates which were given to graduates of the Belfast Ladies' Institute were given little recognition outside Ulster. As a result of this, the lady overseers realised that their classes required official recognition if they were to be of real value to their students. In 1869 the committee, with the addition of Professor Nesbitt and Professor Thomson resolved to hold a general meeting with all the ladies associated with the scheme. The purpose of the gathering was to draw up a memorial to be sent to the senate of the Queen's University of Ireland, requesting that their examinations be officially recognised. The ladies were encouraged in this task by Cambridge University and Trinity College Dublin, which had already drawn up plans for examinations for female students. Pressure from leading girls'-school principals had helped to persuade Cambridge University to open the higher local examinations to girls in 1868.

Mrs Margaret Byers, principal of the Ladies' Collegiate School in Belfast had tried before, without success, to persuade Cambridge to open an examination centre in Belfast where her pupils could sit examinations. The Cambridge University authorities believed that Belfast was too far from Cambridge to make this workable. A similar petition had been sent to Trinity

College Dublin, but the ladies of the institute really preferred Queen's College, one of the three national colleges in Ireland, because this college would be more convenient for their students. The ladies were aware of the fact that the girls would only be awarded certificates, not degrees (this was the practice in other universities), but they were still enthusiastic that the tests should be held. A memorial from the institute was drawn up on 5 October 1869. It said that it would do everything possible to carry out the examinations. The memorial was forwarded by the Belfast Ladies' Institute to the senate of Queen's College, and a scheme for examinations was drawn up in 1869. The ladies started to modify their existing plan of tests to comply with the new Queen's College examinations. It is fortunate that the institute's lecturers were already chosen from Queen's College, thus guaranteeing their high standard.

The secretary of the institute drew up circulars to publicise their new scheme, and the first examinations were held in 1870. In January of that year the secretary of the institute wrote to the university asking for details of when the examinations' regulations would be available. This enabled the Belfast Ladies' Institute to plan for the examinations and organise a post-mortem after the completion of the first tests so that the tests could be evaluated.

There were two sections to university tests: junior and senior. Some subjects were compulsory – for example, English literature and arithmetic. Pupils who passed the junior section could move on to the senior section. The examinations were generally held in June each year, and this was convenient for girls who attended either boarding or day schools in Belfast which had collegiate or university facilities and who went home for the summer holidays.

One feature of these Queen's College examinations was that money prizes and scholarships were awarded. The most successful candidates might win up to £50. These prizes inspired the girls to finish their courses. Prizes were offered to students who took the examinations, and each year a list of the prizewinners was published in the local newspaper. Money prizes and honours certificates were presented for outstanding merit, and other graduates received a university certificate without special rating. At first it was the policy of the senate of the university to maintain as much privacy as possible when publishing results. Candidates were known by numbers, so that the examiners could not identify them, and no class lists were published. However, when some prizes were obtained in the second year of these examinations it was decided that the senate should announce the winners by name. In 1873 those taking honours examinations were published, and in 1874 the names of all the successful candidates were given. No information was given stating where the young ladies had been educated, though at Cambridge this information was given as a matter of course. It is impossible, therefore, to ascertain the number of young ladies taking Queen's College examinations that were taught in the Belfast ladies' Institute.

Early disclosures of honours and details of subjects were requested by some women candidates who were anxious to learn about their own positions. For example, a Mrs T. Reid complained in 1874 that the regulations at the university were issued too late. She pointed out that, for examinations in English literature, the books – Spalding's *Literature*, Marsh's *Lectures*, Morrow's *Accordance with Hamlet*, thirty of Bacon's essays and Hall's *English Poets* – with many notes were only issued in February. As Mrs Reid said, it was not possible to expect anyone to prepare honestly and without cramming for a June examination.

The Belfast Ladies' Institute, over the years, corresponded with the Queen's College senate over changes in examinations, and these requests were favourably regarded. For example, in 1875 the ladies asked the university senate to permit senior candidates to take obligatory subjects in one year and optional ones in the following year. They also requested that any marks gained be held over to the second year to enable subjects to be dealt with separately. French and Latin, they requested, should be added to the list of junior examinations. The senate agreed to these proposals. They also consented to add a new subject, the theory of music, to the senior course – this subject was on the list of examinations held at other universities, and it was regarded as of great use to ladies who wanted to become teachers. It was also regarded as of great use from a scientific point of view, and so it was attractive to the lady overseers of the institute, who were always keen to promote science. They said that the study of musical theory would correct the superficial habits of thought which were particularly prevalent in the study of music. This is an example of the institute's efforts to prove that young ladies were able to cope with their studies. The senate accepted the new course and added 'perspective' to the art examination.

In 1877 the Belfast Ladies' Institute had to approach the senate when they found that the certificates of the university examinations for women were not accepted by the London School of Medicine as an entry qualification. This posed a problem for Ulster girls who hoped to qualify in medicine, for the London School of Medicine was the only educational establishment which admitted women to medical training. It was essential therefore that the Irish certificates should be recognised.

The members of the senate wrote to the General Medical Council in response to the institute's protest. The ladies also wrote to Sir Dominic Corrigan, the university representative on the General Medical Council, in October 1877 complaining about the situation; and in answer to these complaints it was agreed that Irish qualifications would be valid.

In 1879 the Queen's University of Ireland was replaced by the Royal University of Ireland, which, unlike its predecessor, was purely an examining body. The most important aspect of the Royal University of Ireland was that women could take degrees under the same conditions as men – a great step forward for those women that wanted careers. Girls could now become members of the university and take BA and MA degrees. The Belfast Ladies' Institute continued its classes, but it now faced competition from girls' schools, such as the Ladies' Collegiate School, whose principal, Mrs Margaret Byers, prepared a separate department for girls wanting to obtain degrees. The institution continued to be responsible for the sitting of examinations, and Miss Courtney, the institute's secretary, was recommended as the superintendent for the Royal University of Ireland.

The ladies of the institute had complained of a lack of adequate teaching for the girls, and they campaigned to rectify the situation. The institute wrote to the committee of graduates of the Royal University of Ireland in August 1873 mentioning the practical difficulties their organisation faced in regard to increasing awareness of university examinations for women. The letter stressed their hopes of further co-operation in this matter; in fact the ladies of the institute wanted girls to be admitted to university courses. This was now more difficult to attain due to the closure of the Queen's University of Ireland and its replacement with a non-collegiate body. The Belfast Ladies' Institute now concentrated its effort on obtaining the admission of women to other colleges, asking that the colleges do more than hold tests. In September 1873 they wrote to Dr Henry, president of Queen's College Belfast, stressing the need for universities to do as much as possible to help their students. In addition there was in existence a bequest from John Stuart Mill, which would be paid to any university that would admit girls – an added attraction to the authorities.

The requests of the Belfast Ladies' Institute were put off indefinitely. In 1870 the proposal to admit women came before the Queen's College council. Dr Andrews, vice president of the college, and a supporter of the institute, suggested that women should be permitted to attend lectures if the professors were satisfied that discipline in the classes would not suffer. Much discussion took place concerning this matter, and, although there was some support, it was not possible to convince some of the professors that the admission of girls was practical. There seemed to be little chance that Queen's College would lead the way in women's education despite pressure from the Belfast Ladies' Institute. Professor Nesbitt proposed a motion in regard to women students in 1873 during a convocation meeting. The institute itself forwarded another memorandum to the senate. Sir Thomas McClure, MP, and Mr Pim, MP, whose wife served on the committee, supported the demands of the ladies. There was no need of further help from the other universities.

To obtain teachers capable of raising the level of education among the ladies, more efficient aid was necessary; only the best scholars were able to go forward from the schools to university examinations, but the process was so slow that it could not make any wide impression. Without public or permanent schools, without intellectual training, it was impossible for women to have a good education, and it was now acknowledged that they should, but only the universities offered the highest kind of instruction. Queen's College was hampered by traditional rules. It was in harmony with the accepted thinking of the times, but degrees had to be opened up to women if society was to move with the times.

The ladies of the institute then offered a compromise. The institute wrote to the university stating that if medical classes were formed they would state their conviction that separate instruction in the subjects was absolutely essential under the rules of the university. The senate considered this application and referred the matter to the law officers of the Crown to ascertain whether they possessed the power to make decisions. The senate, however, was informed that this was outside their jurisdiction.

In 1874 the entire question of the legality of admitting women to Queen's College was considered in order to clarify the position of the girls who had been trying to gain admission. A memorial was again prepared, but the fall of Gladstone's government meant that it was never forwarded. Supporters of higher education for women in no way compelled universities to admit them; indeed a letter from Isabella Tod to the institute in April 1874 emphasised this. It was clear that if Irish universities did take steps to admit women, they were at liberty to do so in whatever way they pleased. An enabling bill enabled any university to do what it thought best, without being bound by old rules and regulations.

In 1882 the Belfast Ladies' Institute once again wrote to the president of Queen's College to request his support for their efforts to advance the cause of further and higher education for women – especially to those that passed the matriculation examination and needed tuition for a BA. There were some ladies schools offering advanced classes, but the institute firmly believed that honours degrees were very desirable for their students. This time the institute was successful, and the first women entered upon their studies for a BA in 1882.

This achievement was not obtained solely through the petitions and demands of the ladies, although these were important. By the 1880s it was becoming harder to discriminate against women with regard to higher education; primary and secondary schools were educating and examining both sexes equally.

It is possible that the Royal University of Ireland was happy to have intelligent young women to swell the student numbers, though certainly during the 1880s some of the principals of the girls' schools feared that they would suffer from 'poaching' by the men's colleges.

There was further progress in 1889 when women were admitted to Queen's College to medical lectures, and in the following year to classes in all faculties. In 1895 the government altered the status of the Royal University of Ireland to make women equal to men in the competition for scholarships. Only a small number of girls went to Queen's College; much larger numbers continued to attend the college departments of girls' schools. The headmistresses' fears of 'poaching' appear to have been unjustified.

Only a few women took advantage of the new openings in higher education, but these women were considered as pioneers and role models for younger girls.

The business of the Belfast Ladies' Institute was not confined to tertiary-level educational provisions for women. The emphasis was upon the teaching of young girls aged between sixteen and eighteen who had already received some education, either at home or in the many ladies' seminaries. The committee was also interested in teaching standards, for standards had an important effect on subsequent academic attainments. The report of the Endowed Schools' Commission in 1868 highlighted the inadequate state of education for upper- and middle-class girls in England. No report was produced in Ireland, but provisions were no better.

The Belfast Ladies' Institute was well aware of the inadequacy of the supported public schools, so they petitioned the House of Commons in June 1873. According to the existing provisions, only girls in the National Schools had the opportunity to take public examinations, and the ladies were concerned about the subsequent poor quality of education for girls. The lack of secondary-level testing reinforced their opinion that there were inadequate means of study for girls. There were no public endowments in Belfast for girls for any opportunity other than primary education. In 1878 the Tory government reacted to demands for secondary education in Ireland by introducing the Intermediate Education (Ireland) Bill, which proposed to establish a system of education supported by public funds. The supporters of higher education for women were delighted at this suggestion, which would provide opportunities for girls. Fearing that the girls would not benefit from the intermediate system, the Belfast Ladies' Institute drew up another memorial addressed to the Lord Chancellor, Lord Cairns, and to James Lowther, the Chief

Secretary for Ireland, dated 25 June 1878. It stated that women of the middle and upper classes should have a recognised regime, as well as the men of those classes. It stated that education for boys in Ireland had been neglected, and was even more neglected for girls. The endowments of which they could claim a share were scanty. The entire support of higher education had been left to private enterprise, which was local and limited in extent. They brought this matter before the Chief Secretary for Ireland, but no opportunity presented itself for taking any satisfactory action upon it.

The question was so important that the Belfast Ladies' Institute sent a deputation of Irishwomen to London to lobby Lord Cairns. This deputation was organised by Isabella Tod, with the assistance of J. P. Corry, a Belfast Member of Parliament. This provided an opportunity for the women to state their case and emphasise women's achievements in university certificate examinations. The Lord Chancellor was impressed by their arguments and admitted girls under the provision of the Act. Corry was a strong supporter of education for young girls, and he was delighted that the Education Act had been extended to the whole instead of half of the young people of Ireland.

The Belfast Ladies' Institute suspected that the commissioners of education might be reluctant to apply the Act. In the event of any delay, the women planned to send a second deputation to Dublin to press for action and to call a public meeting. Their caution was unfounded, for Mrs Byers of Victoria College Belfast, and Mrs Jellicoe of Alexandra College, Dublin, made sure that the pupils took their examinations in the first year.

This Act was a landmark in the history of education. Although boys and girls were examined separately, the tests were of equal difficulty and were marked on the same level. For the first time girls were shown to be as competent as boys. The university examinations were important, but they never embraced a substantial proportion of the population. With the Intermediate

Education Act female education blossomed through the middle classes, and the Belfast Ladies' Institute played a crucial role in this achievement.

The institute on the whole was a successful organisation. During its first session in 1867–8 there had been over 180 students enrolled, and the professors at Queen's College had earned large fees.

The lady overseers were shocked to receive a letter from Professor Younger in September 1868, withdrawing his agreement to hold classes in the latest sessions. His decision had been prompted by a warning from the president of the university, Dr P. S. Henry, while delivering lectures to the Belfast Ladies' Institute. This might contradict Younger's claim that he had not realised the extent of the commitment required to lecture at the Belfast Ladies' Institute. The lady overseers replied that Professor Nesbitt had allowed lectures before. The professors, they said, were impossible to replace at short notice, and, as several lectures would have to be cancelled, this would damage a valuable institution, which was conducted in the same way as Queen's College and other universities. The ladies therefore asked the president to reconsider the matter, for, they said, it was vital that this issue should be settled promptly and a favourable decision be reached in order to maintain the institute's credibility. It was essential that the Queen's College professors, with their high teaching status, should continue to lecture. Moreover, it was bad for the entire enterprise if they were forced to cancel classes that had already been advertised and paid for.

The president of Queen's College ignored the situation for a while. The ladies circulated copies of the president's letter to the professors to inform them of the risks of fulfilling their teaching agreements with the institute. This was a controversial issue for the president, for Queen's College faced considerable opposition from the gentlemen whose families were associated with the institute and whose views were solicited on the issue. For example,

Mr Dunville and Mr Duffin formed a deputation to visit the president.

On 29 September the president wrote an official letter to the institute stating that if he had been consulted, he would only have permitted staff to teach their own subjects and not to deliver the other twenty-five lectures. Henry concluded that if these conditions were met, he would not interfere further, but he asked that all future plans would be submitted to him first.

Now Professor Wyville Thomson wrote to the Queen's College president from the Commission of Science and Art in Dublin. Thomson had received a letter from Miss Connery of the Belfast Ladies' Institute explaining the situation. Thomson declared that the Belfast Ladies' Institute was a popular, useful body that brought staff into contact with a cross-section of Belfast's population. Thomson highlighted the fact that a number of influential people had supported the institute, and that it was part of a wider educational movement already existing in Edinburgh, Dublin and other leading cities. Thomson felt that the president's right to interfere in the spare time of his staff was questionable. He said that he was entitled, when his college work for the day had been done, to give a lecture if he chose to the Belfast Ladies' Institute, and to give a further lecture to working men. He could write articles for a journal, or take a hand at whist.

The correspondence between Thomson and the Queen's College president continued until Thomson advised Dr Henry that it was not a good idea to interfere with agreements made between professors and the Belfast Ladies' Institute. Professors, he said, should only be reprimanded if they were neglecting their duties. In October 1868 the president conceded, but an unfortunate result of this dispute was that the institute's classes for the 1868 session had to be cancelled; fees already paid had to be refunded. However, the existence of the institute was not in question.

The institute faced similar difficulties with the Government School of Art in October 1872 over the teachers' contractual arrangements. This led to the suspension of classes on the history and principles of art. The following year the institute had to renegotiate their arrangements with the Belfast Natural History and Philosophical Society over the use of the museum premises. This was resolved in a friendly manner, and by March 1874 committee meetings of the institute were again being held in the museum free of charge.

These occurrences provided an interesting example of the influence of the lady overseers – an influence that led to victory over important figures, like the president of Queen's College Belfast.

By the 1880s the existence of the Belfast Ladies' Institute had come into question. The organisation had questioned its future position as early as February 1878, when the ladies discussed the desirability of continuing lectures under the control of the institute; the ladies thought other subjects might be of advantage to them. The entire position of girls' education had come into question. Women were by now admitted to all educational establishments. Intermediate examinations had encouraged the opening of secondary schools throughout Ireland. The existence of collegiate department in colleges, and the opening of Queen's College, Belfast classes to girls, had removed the necessity of outside bodies. Meetings of the institute were only held annually, and in some years they were not held at all, reflecting a decline in activity. By 1883 the committee of the institute had to admit their inability to provide courses and to organise a memorial scholarship for the late Mrs Jane McIlwaine, who had been one of their founders. A group of ladies of the Ladies' Collegiate School had formed an association to encourage girls to attend the collegiate classes of their old school. The Belfast Ladies' Institute believed that this group was in the best position to raise funds. The institute decided to give a corporate subscription to McIlwaine's memorial to show that their friend was appreciated in Belfast.

In April 1897 the final meeting of the Belfast Ladies' Institute was held. Lady Ewart presided, with only three members present. It was agreed that the remaining funds of the institute should go to the Isabella Tod Memorial Scholarship. Their final resolution was that as the object for which the Belfast Ladies' Institute was founded had been accomplished – the goal of higher education for women – the association should be formally disbanded.

The Belfast Ladies' Institute played an important role in Ulster, forging links with women's educational reform movements in Britain and Ireland – for example, the Women's Educational Union and the Edinburgh Association. Isabella Tod, as early as January 1872, seconded the motion, along with Anna Wellard, that the National Union for the Improvement of the Education of Women should be open to all classes. On 25 August 1874 the institute held a meeting at the Ladies' Collegiate School in Belfast in connection with the National Union for the Improvement of the Higher Education of Women. It was chaired by Lord Waveney, and addressed by Mr G. Johnston Stoney and Mrs William Grey, who travelled to Belfast as representatives of the union. In May 1880 the overseers of the Belfast Ladies' Institute attended a meeting of the committee of the Society for School and University Education for Women in Ireland. They were instructed to use their own judgement, and make decisions as the situation demanded. In May 1882 Isabella Tod was awarded travelling expenses by the Belfast Ladies' Institute so that she could go to London on important business concerning girls and the Intermediate Education Board.

All these organisations provided education for middle-class women. Members of the Belfast Ladies' Institute were strong advocates of the advancement of the social position of women, and together they made a formidable group. The organisation played a key role in determining a woman's right to education in the fast-expanding city of Belfast.

Chapter 3

Political Ambitions

Young Ireland was a term given to a band of nationalists formed around *The Nation* newspaper. In 1846 they broke away from O'Connell's movement, and in 1847 they formed the Irish Confederates. A rebellion was attempted in 1848, but it quickly collapsed. *The Nation* was based in Dublin, but Young Irelanders came from all parts of the island, and a large number of their leaders came from the northern counties. For instance, Charles Gavan Duffy came from Monaghan and John Mitchel came from Londonderry.

Northern women from two families were involved: the Mitchel women and the Hughes sisters – Margaret Hughes Callan and Susan Hughes, who became Charles Gavan Duffy's second wife. Along with these there was Elizabeth Treacy, better known in Young Ireland circles as Finola, who was a frequent contributor to *The Nation*. These women were among the leading Young Ireland activists.

It is important to determine whether or not the role of the Northern Young Ireland women was different from that of their male counterparts. Were they in any way influenced by the environment? What was the reason for their interest in nationalism?

To help in this examination, it is useful to look at the female environment of the Young Irelanders in general, and also to examine the attitude in the north of Ireland, before looking at the individual lives of the women.

Women, of course, played a leading role in nationalism in Ulster, but their contributions are often overlooked. Young Irelanders were often the contributors of prose, poetry and editorials in *The Nation*, the *United Irishman*, the *Irish Felon* and the *Irish Tribune*. They were also important for their support of a group attending meetings of the Repeal Association. They cheered speakers on and observed court cases. When the Irish Confederation was formed, women were among its members, but the majority of these women remained in the background and did not take part in the committee meetings. However, there were always women that influenced the decision-making process through their informal contacts with the small circle of Young Ireland leaders, especially as wives and relatives and close friends.

Revolution in Europe attracted the attention of the Irish Confederation in 1848, when many of its members talked about the possibility of an Irish uprising. Male Young Irelanders were arrested for publishing articles, and female work became essential, particularly in maintaining communication between members.

As a whole it is difficult to trace the movements of women in the Young Ireland movement, because attention was mainly on the men, but some information does exist. The poetesses have left plenty of material to examine, and in *The Nation* there was also a long debate in 1847–8 about the role of women.

Women had a key role to play in the national movement. They were not chosen to be leaders, but they were considered important in spreading the nationalist message through the education of children. Women liked this since it gave them a sense of belonging and identified them as important in the nationalist movement, but these women cannot be seen as feminists since their nationalism took priority over such issues as political equality.

In 1848 a large number of women demanded a more active role. They wanted to take part in revolt. This received some support from the male Young Irelanders, who thought that a national revolution would require the participation of both sexes. Since the uprising never occurred on a large scale, their willingness to include women was never properly tested.

The Young Irelanders were eager to win Protestant support for the repeal movement, but they were aware of the religious tensions within the province. Articles in *The Nation* addressed this subject for northern Protestants. They did not see the north as a separate problem; it was put in the context of the general alienation of Protestants from Irish nationalism. A distinction was drawn between Orangemen and Protestants – Orangeism was regarded as a misled ideology. They believed that Protestants, north and south, would eventually support an independent parliament if they thought that they would benefit from it. This meant that Protestants would start to regard Ireland as their own country. This belief also derived from the activities of the Young Irelanders. For example, Anglicans, like Thomas Davis, William Smith O'Brien and Jane Francesca Elgee, and Unitarians like John and Jenny Mitchel, were keen nationalists and believed that others might follow the nationalist path. Young Ireland was strongly secular and demanded unity of class and creed, but Catholics from the north, like Charles Gavan Duffy from Monaghan, remembered from their childhood how deep the divisions were. Duffy and others were critical of the idealist view that northern Protestants would join the nationalist movement, but many Young Irelanders believed that Protestants realised that consecutive British governments had played Catholics and Protestants off against each other for political purposes.

Young Irelanders were convinced that Protestants were too strong a minority to be oppressed by Catholics in an independent Irish parliament. The Young Irelanders praised northern Protestants for their thrift, industry, discipline, strength of character and courage. They praised their good spirit of co-operation, their strict adherence to principle and their independence of thought. On the other hand, they considered that the Protestants had been deceived by Britain, although this contradicted their own view of an independent spirit in the province. There were indications that Protestants generally respected Young Ireland more than O'Connell, and they viewed them as more honest, and straightforward and secular.

Young Ireland used precedents to show that unity of creed was possible, and emphasis was placed on economic arguments to win Protestants over to the cause. Young Ireland, however, did not see any economic benefits in the Act of Union. Many Young Irelanders realised that the north was different from the south, for in the north there was a lot of industry. They did not realise how strongly Unionists supported the Union. They said that there would be no reversal of the seventeenth-century plantations, and they stressed the point that Protestants in Ireland had a right to their holdings, since they had lived in the country for so long. They also praised the so-called Ulster Custom as a way forward for Ireland. But Protestant landlords feared for their property, in spite of Young Ireland assurances to the contrary.

Since Young Ireland found it difficult to relate to the lower classes, they did not understand the fears of the Protestant working classes. In 1848 John Mitchel abandoned the appeals aimed at the Protestant ascendancy, and in his newspaper, the *United Irishman*, he directed proclamations to the farmers, labourers and artisans of Ulster. He said that England had plundered both Catholic and Protestant farmers in Ireland, and he asked them to join the nationalist movement to arrest this exploitation.

All these appeals could not overcome the divisions in Ulster. Repeal agitation had sparked a rise in Orangeism, making O'Connell reluctant to hold large meetings in Ulster.

The Young Irelanders were very interested in the north and campaigned in the province. As in the rest of Ireland, the Irish Confederation was active there. The Young Irelanders came from mainly respectable families, and the arrest of John Mitchel and John Martin in 1848 caused great surprise and hostility among their northern neighbours.

Ulsterwomen within the Young Irelanders shared the mainstream of Young Ireland thought in the north, but they also had their own ideas.

John Mitchel came from a respectable family. He was the son of the Reverend John Mitchel and Mary Mitchel, who had four daughters and two sons. All had strong independent personalities, and the women never shrank away from danger. This attitude probably originated with the Mitchel parents. In their home, all the Mitchels were involved in talks about books, politics and religion. Mary Mitchel had always worked in her husband's parish, and she was a remarkable person. When the Reverend John Mitchel died in 1840, she successfully ran the Mitchel household along with her daughters. She was described as very intelligent, witty and fiery – a very forceful character. She had an excellent understanding of business and management. Whenever John and Jenny needed assistance because of their involvement in the Young Ireland movement, the Mitchel women rallied around them. In her support of John and Jenny, Mary Mitchel travelled a great deal. She moved to Dublin, and, after John was transported, she decided to emigrate to the United States. Hearing about her resolution, John wrote to his sister Matilda. She was surprised at her mother's decision to emigrate.

Mary lived in America for several years, but after a while went to live in London, before moving back to Newry, where she died in 1865.

John's sister Matilda was near him in age, and closest in confidence. John wrote frequently to her and trusted her without question. She appears to have been an intelligent woman. She had a passion for books. Two of his sisters, Mary and Henrietta, stayed many times with John and Jenny in their home in Dublin during the Young Ireland period. Only Henrietta remained closely involved in politics.

Jenny Mitchel was the most active female in the Young Irelanders, but the moral support of all the Mitchel women was significant.

Jane (Jenny) Verner was born in the Newry area in 1820. By the age of sixteen she had eloped twice with John Mitchel, and she eventually married him on 3 February 1837. The couple lived with her family in Newry, and John was made very welcome. He was quickly made part of the household. In 1840 John and Jenny moved to Banbridge, where John practised as a country attorney.

Jenny was strong, independent and gentle. She was more a partner to John than a subservient housewife.

Once John and Jenny had become interested in the ideas mentioned in *The Nation* and in the Young Ireland group, politics started to dominate their lives. Duffy offered John Mitchel the post of assistant editor of *The Nation* in 1845, but Jenny was opposed to the idea of John changing his profession.

Once the family had moved to Dublin, Jenny became a full participant in political activities. The Mitchel home became the centre of Young Ireland activities. John was occupied with his newspaper, and he relied heavily upon his organisational skills to manage the family affairs. In their home, simplicity and frugality combined with neatness were the main features. They had to exist on a tight budget, but Jenny was able to stretch her meagre income and thus ensure they could fulfil their social obligations. The suppers which she hosted for Young Ireland activities may be compared to European-style salons, where the ladies took command when politics was mentioned.

Mary Mitchel and her daughters were keen visitors before

Henrietta, Mary and William moved permanently to Dublin at the end of 1846. All the Mitchels gave John their full support. For instance, Jenny and the Mitchel sisters attended meetings of the Repeal Association in Conciliation Hall, where, together with other women, they sat in the gallery. Women were also invited to banquets of the '82 Club, a select group modelled on the Irish Volunteers in 1782, and it is likely that some of the Mitchel women were present.

Jenny read newspapers to assist John in his work, and she kept clippings for future reference. John Mitchel left the Irish Confederation and he was dependent on his family's support. All the Mitchel women wrote anonymous articles and letters, edited contributions, read newspapers and undertook essential work to make the journal a success.

Like John, Jenny was full of ideas, and she too believed in the necessity of revolution in Ireland. Her husband included women in his plans and even assigned them a role in combat. The strong position of women in his family must have influenced his opinions in the nationalist movement.

John was arrested and sentenced to transportation in May 1848 for writing seditous articles. Jenny attempted to rally opposition to John's arrest and transportation, but she failed. Many nationalists saw her as a symbol of oppressed Ireland. A special committee was established for the collection of funds for John Mitchel and his children.

Jenny was extremely disappointed when John was convicted. However, her involvement in the Young Ireland movement continued, for she helped Thomas Devin Reilly to escape to the United States. Jenny wanted to leave Ireland as soon as possible to join her husband, and she was the only woman that followed a Young Irelander into the penal colonies. She was depressed about the failure of the Young Ireland rebellion, and the bleak condition of affairs in Ireland.

The Mitchel family also experienced difficulties after John's transportation. In an undated letter, Jenny mentioned that her correspondence had been tampered with.

John's final destination was uncertain, and he worried a good deal about Jenny's desire to follow him, believing that she might not be physically fit for a three-month voyage. He repeatedly wrote to his sister and said that Jenny should not travel.

Once John's destination had been decided upon, Jenny and her family followed him to Van Diemen's Land (Tasmania). When John decided to escape to the United States, Jenny assisted him, while at the same time organising her own flight.

In America she helped John on his various newspapers and remained interested in the Irish nationalist cause, but John and Jenny felt an emptiness in their lives when they realised that their cause had failed. Young Ireland activities had been the centre of their lives, and nothing could replace the excitement of the Young Ireland years.

Jenny was a Unitarian, and she was very tolerant. She allowed two of her daughters to become Roman Catholics.

When Jenny visited Ireland in 1862–3 she decided to bring back goods to the blockaded states. She and her daughter travelled back on a blockade-breaker, which ran aground and caught fire. They were left stranded on a sandy island near the coast of North Carolina, but they were able to make their way home to Richmond after great difficulty and hardship.

In 1875 John was asked to stand as a home-rule candidate for Tipperary, despite the fact that he was opposed to the home-rule movement, but he travelled to Ireland for the elections and Jenny was eager to accompany him.

John was elected, but he died shortly afterwards. Jenny Mitchel did not actively campaign for Irish nationalism after her husband's death, but she remained interested in Irish politics until her death on 31 December 1899.

Unlike Jenny Mitchel, Henrietta Mitchel Martin, John's youngest sister, was highly involved in the home-rule movement. She began her career in the Young Ireland movement, and she frequently visited John and Jenny in Dublin before moving there permanently. Henrietta helped the couple in Young Ireland activities, and she attended repeal meetings before the split in 1846. She was also engaged in writing articles for the *United Irishman*.

After the unsuccessful rebellion of 1848 she remained a strong Young Ireland supporter and continue to follow their ideas.

To the surprise of many friends and relatives, she married John Mitchel's best friend, a fellow Young Irelander, John Martin, on 26 November 1868. It appeared to be a happy marriage. She followed her husband to the United States and shared his political views. She was a busy woman and encouraged the quiet Martin to become involved in politics again, and to follow the path of the home-rule movement. Upon their return to Ireland he became home-rule MP for Meath from 1871 to 1875 and secretary of the Irish Home Rule League from 1874 to 1875.

Henrietta also remained loyal to her brother, and she was involved in his election campaign in 1875. She did not see her involvement in the election as a breach with the Young Ireland tradition. She looked upon the fight for home rule as a continuance of the Young Ireland struggle for an independent Irish parliament.

Her husband died in 1875, and she wrote to George Mahon, outlining a strong nationalist case. She was also aware of Protestant representation in the home-rule party.

She then took a break from politics, and, in the spring of 1876, a friend asked her if she would assist a Unitarian minister with his work in Milan. She felt that she had no vocation, although she wanted to leave Ireland, for she felt depressed after the death of her husband and her brother.

She returned to Ireland in May or June 1877, and she continued working in John Martin's name for the home-rule movement. She supported the politics of Parnell, and, after the split in the home-rule movement, she remained a strong Parnellite. She travelled widely to obtain support for the home-rule cause, and her name appeared frequently in nationalist meetings. For example, in 1903 she attended the Irish League Convention in Boston in the United States, where she met John Redmond, John Dillon and Michael Davitt.

It is interesting to note that all her activities were dedicated to her dead husband and his nationalist cause. She never claimed to work for herself, and this attitude reflects her own romantic nationalism.

Henrietta Mitchel Martin died on 11 July 1913 in her house in Dublin. She was buried in Newry.

Margaret Hughes was born about 1817, and her sister Susan, the fifth daughter of a large Catholic family, was born on 19 August 1826. Their grandmother had been a strong Irish nationalist, and it is likely that their interest in the movement derived from their family. When their father, Philip Hughes, died, Margaret and her mother started a boarding school in Dublin in 1835. After a while Susan and the other sisters taught in the school, which was advertised in *The Nation*. Susan also gave piano lessons in 1846. By then, Margaret was already married to Dr John B. Callan, who also advertised his selection of mineral waters in *The Nation*. Although Margaret Callan became involved in Young Ireland and worked on *The Nation*, it is not recorded what her duties were. Like most women of the time, Margaret was not in the forefront of attention, despite working hard for the Young Ireland movement.

Most articles in *The Nation* were published without credit to the author, and only two have been positively attributed to her: 'A Day at Versailles' and 'A Day in Paris'. Both appeared in 1843 and were travel articles. She said that she was in France at the time they were written, and they were intended to heighten people's national consciousness and show how the people of other nations love their countries. She wrote that the English had left no national monuments, but the movement could create them. Why should we not have a national monument, she asked, where the deeds done by her countrymen could be preserved to instruct the present and future generations. She had reported to the Conservatoire in Paris and stressed the benefits of a national government of Ireland which would be able to support a good educational system and create the opportunity for Irishmen to improve themselves. Events where foreigners supported the women were also mentioned in the articles. When Margaret met a Frenchman on the bus in Paris there were remarks about the beauty of the scenery, but they also talked of Ireland's aspirations for liberty (upon which, he said, the eyes of his country were riveted) and of the generous support of the French people, who of course had much experience of revolution dating back to the end of the eighteenth century. These travel reports were perhaps the first female writings of length published in *The Nation*. They are undoubtedly first-hand accounts, and they provide an interesting picture of Margaret Callan as a well-educated and sophisticated woman.

Under the pen name of Thornton MacMahon she went on to edit *The Casket of Irish Pearls*, a collection of works by Irish authors, in 1846. In the introduction she pointed out the necessity of studying the works of writers other than English authors, who were sometimes critical of Ireland. By learning about Irish history, culture and literature, she said, young people could learn about their country and gain self-respect as natives of Ireland. Like other Young Irelanders she also pleaded with her readers to overcome disunity. This was extremely important for her as an Ulsterwoman. The armies of enemies would be overcome to frustrate the policy of disunion that they had so long and so justly reckoned upon. Had their fathers listened in their day to this holy preaching of mutual love and mutual charity, instead of listening to insane bigotry, how changed a destiny might they have left their children, she argued. Discussing the historical writing in this book, she saw what successive British governments had done in Ireland. She blamed England for religious divisions in Ulster. The Penal Laws, she said, were designed to make disunity among the Irish, but she was quick to cite examples in Irish history where all believers came together to worship Christ. The government, she said, was forcing upon the people certain brass halfpence – a scheme at which much of Swift's ridicule had been levelled. This is remembered because it had an intrinsic importance for Catholics, Protestants and Presbyterians, who combined against the government. The result of this was triumph for Ireland. Fear shook the English quarters lest this intimacy might stir into friendship, and so melt away the prejudices which they had so far carefully nurtured. She argued that England could only govern Ireland when the country was divided. Once the Irish people united, they could obtain self-government, but this, she said, required a good education. She said the national education might overcome prejudice, though bigotry and ignorance still held strong in the north, and no power or education could ever dislodge them. The pen, she said, was mightier than the sword as a weapon to wield against prejudice.

Margaret Callan appears to have been a moral nationalist. In 1848 she followed Duffy's moderate ideas rather than Mitchel's extremism.

Callan had not much to say about women. Her blood was dedicated to the young men of Ireland and she had hope for the coming years. Three female writers were at work – Mrs Tighe, Lady Morgan and Miss Edgeworth – but Margaret Callan expressed a low opinion of aristocratic ladies. Who had not heard of the schemes for the improvement of the peasantry in matters of farming, cleanliness, etc., which had failed? Sometimes the cause of failure of such schemes was easily traceable: for example, when a landlord offered a new faith along with comforts; or when a utopian community which some of the ladies had planned occupied their minds for a brief season until that caprice was set aside for some other novel idea. Margaret Callan felt that these wealthy women performed charitable work because they were bored. She said that the root of all evil lay in the lack of understanding between landlords and tenants. In her view, nationalism could overcome great divisions in the classes. The desire to improve conditions in Ireland would encourage co-operation among all classes, she said, and the Irish should rely upon their own strengths, skills and unity. Through a good education the miserable condition of the people would be relieved.

Margaret Callan viewed nationalism as a unifying force that would unite all classes and creeds. Her beliefs were centred in the Young Ireland movement.

Margaret's sister Susan met Charles Gavan Duffy in Young Ireland circles and eventually married him in February 1847. Subsequently she paid much attention to her home. She had been an excellent pianist – she had studied under Chopin and Liszt – but she gave up the piano because Duffy did not like it. She also gave up her work in the school. However, she still played an important role in supporting her husband and nationalism. It is not known if she wrote political works.

During the revolutionary activities of 1848 Margaret's work in the Young Ireland movement became more important. When Duffy and other leading members of the movement were arrested, Margaret worked to continue the publication of *The Nation*. She worked mainly in the editor's room, and others wrote most of the articles. However, the police seized the types, manuscripts and proofs and closed the paper down.

Margaret seems to have passed on the spirit of the Young Ireland movement. Two of her former pupils volunteered to act as messengers for the Irish Confederation leaders when communication broke down during the revolutionary year of 1848. She believed that the mission was too dangerous for young women and she refused to send them to the troubled counties.

The revolution failed, but Margaret and Susan remained in communication with many Young Irelanders, even though some of their families had emigrated to Australia in 1855–6.

In September 1878, Susan Duffy died of tuberculosis after a long illness. Margaret died in Melbourne about 1883.

Elizabeth Treacy was born at Ballymena. She came from a Protestant landowning family. Her two sisters married between 1848 and 1859, but Elizabeth remained single for some time and lived with her mother in Ballymena. O'Sullivan, in his book on Young Ireland, placed her amongst the six most important females in the Young Irelanders. She did not contribute regularly to *The Nation* before 1848; only from the 1850s did she regularly write patriotic verses in the paper under the pen name of Finola. It appears that Finola was not in personal contact with the Young Irelanders in Dublin, but she was acquainted with other northern women involved in the movement.

She wrote to William Smith O'Brien in 1858, claiming to be a distant kinsman of his. She told him that patriotism in Ulster was still alive and that the people still hoped that Ireland's nationalism would last. The time was now at hand to organise a spirited national party. She asked Smith O'Brien to form an Irish party, and she invited him to visit her if he was in Ulster. She was a Protestant and supported the desire of the northern Catholics to see Ireland emerge from the degraded state it was in.

Finola's poetry was not extremist. She strongly asserted her nationalist beliefs, but she looked at people's social circumstances, such as their poverty, rather than writing about blood and violence. Her poems were often sad but tender, depicting the results of social decline. She wrote about the circumstances of people in the workhouses or in low-paid jobs, whose happy memories of the past were their only remaining consolation. Her 'heroes' were the socially disadvantaged industrial workers, impoverished women, poor children, and the victims of evictions and forced emigration. Her work reflects the poverty of Ulster from the 1850s. Finola also employed powerful symbols, and many of her images were connected with natural catastrophes such as storms and shipwrecks. Women and girls were a particular feature of the poems, and their difficult destiny and suffering is recorded in great detail.

For example, in 'Only a Factory Child' she wrote about a factory girl. Nature here served as an escape from hardship. The factory child was set free from her daily toil to bask for a few hours in the light of freedom. The child was depicted with 'the brow of age . . . sad, and worn; a waif from the city's streets, unfriended and forlorn'. She dreamed of 'the far-off sea, the wild waves' murmuring strain – the crash of the spectral wheels still throbbing through her brain'. A few brief happy hours were spent 'away from the dismal street; through the shadowy lane she hastes with childhood's willing feet'.

Finola tried not to idealise poverty. Her female heroines were not the unassuming, beautiful, poor women of fantasy, but, rather, strong, stubborn and tough people. In 'Rosaleen' her heroine depicted Erin in a most unusual manner. Whereas the Young Irelander James Clarence Mangan idealised his country in his poem 'Roisin Dubh', Finola's Rosaleen did not sigh and weep; nor did she want to be rescued. She challenged her oppressors: 'Rosaleen listened, struck dumb with scorn: only a flash of the downcast eye, only the gust of a stifled sigh, a tremulous flutter of a pulsing heart, a clench of the hand and a sudden start – told how the blow was borne.' Many sided with the weak, and repulsed the strong.

The important question in Finola's poem was why it was not thought womanly to fight for a troubled country – a question that had been previously asked by Mary and Eva in 1848. The women are portrayed as very powerful throughout the poem.

The Young Ireland women wished to contribute to the struggle, and they considered themselves an important part of the nationalist cause, but this did not mean that they demanded equal power.

Finola also included criminals amongst the underprivileged, and she showed sympathy with their plight. In 'Convict's Flower' she asks, 'Who may tell the dark temptations . . . with no light to guide them onward, with no hand to point the way?' It was easy to condemn, she said, boasting of virtue, but 'have you e'er been tried like them?'

This attitude stood in stark contrast to the moralising views of some Young Irelanders, who looked down on lower-class criminals and condemned them for their deeds.

Finola's poems also included the desire to unite people and to overcome social injustice. Her collection of poems entitled *Never Forsake the Ship, and Other Poems*, published in 1874, was dedicated to all creeds and classes. She felt solidarity with the people, and, unlike many Young Irelanders who referred only to the middle classes when talking about 'the people', she also included the lower classes.

In 'Proudly We Stand in the People's Ranks' she demanded equal rights for all. 'We dare', she wrote, 'to preach forth the branded creed of equal rights to all.' On the evil and just the rain would fall. Their weapons would be true thought and fearless speech. With these they would overthrow each low device and base pretence, each aim of the crafty foe. 'Their senseless barricade of words our arms will soon lay waste,' she wrote.

She believed in moral force, not physical force, to master inequality.

In the same poem she also combined religious faith and social issues, and claimed that true religion did not breed inequality. She wrote that it was best to 'rend the tyrant chains that custom forged' and recant the impious creed that resulted in separate laws for rich and poor. It was best to remember who sat at the publican's feet. What jewelled garter or diamond star did those guests, so honoured, wear?

She strongly opposed religious hypocrisy, and in her poem

'Laborare est Orare' she attacked people who pretended to be pious but did nothing to help others in trouble.

Her words transcended classes and creeds; this was a doctrine, pure and simple, that the simplest mind could understand.

Finola lived in Ulster longer than any of the other female Young Irelanders, and she was in closest contact with the social developments there. She stressed the importance of the mushrooming working classes. Like Henrietta Mitchel Martin, she also focused on the recruitment of Protestants into the home-rule cause, which became difficult with the rise of organised Unionism. Finola reflected a different kind of northern identity in her writing. She was both Protestant and a nationalist, as well as sympathising with social issues and industrial workers. She became interested in the Fenian movement, and she campaigned for the release of Fenian prisoners. She wrote a letter to Gladstone on the subject. She became involved in the Land League and the home-rule cause.

Finola addressed movements in Ireland and England on these issues. On 12 September she addressed meetings organised by the Belfast branch of the Irish National League under the chairmanship of Joseph Biggar in St Mary's Hall, Belfast on the subject of 'Ireland As It Is – North and South'. Here she stressed the importance of the land question. She condemned the present land tenure as adverse to every humanitarian principle, and she demanded that land should be inherited by everyone. She urged all the Irish people to support home rule. In her writings her strong religious principles are evident. She said that the earth was God's; there was no respect of persons with God. Divine law had ordained that the husbandman should first enjoy the fruits of his labour. Charles Stewart Parnell was mentioned, as were the coercion laws and Irish landlords. She advised that everyone should lead a holy life and try to the best of their ability to redress the fallen condition of Ireland. Her preoccupation with social issues derived from her strong faith.

Her ideal of a just society was based on her belief in a just God who had created equality.

She married Ralph Varian in 1871. He had been actively involved in Young Ireland through the Cork Citizens Confederate Club. After her wedding she moved to Blackrock, County Cork, and she was very happy with her loving husband; but she did not lose contact with her home, and she travelled frequently to Ulster.

The death of her husband and subsequent financial troubles caused her great distress. She was used to wealth, but she was now cast into poverty and she had to write begging letters to prominent and literary nationalists. In the letters, written about 1893, she claimed to be recovering from an illness and on the edge of starvation and eviction. She hated the idea of going to the poorhouse. She said she remained a nationalist and hoped that the Irish people would not have forgotten Finola, who had always worked on their behalf. The letters are painful reading. Her nationalism was the only thing that she had left. Loneliness and the fear of being forgotten by her audience was harder to shoulder than poverty. She signed the letters 'Finola' as well as with her full name, so that people would remember her.

She died in St Patrick's Hospital, Cork, in 1896, aged seventy-five.

The northern women in Young Ireland came from various religious and social backgrounds, and their lives developed in different directions after the Young Ireland movement had broken up. They did not form a distinct group amongst the female Young Irelanders. Many of them moved to Dublin, but later emigrated from Ireland, and they never focused on a specific northern agenda in their writings. All Young Irelanders were influenced by their upbringing in an island that was divided over religion. All were concerned about the situation in the north. Young Ireland, with its emphasis upon unity of all the Irish people, appealed to them. Ulster nationalists were also able to contribute their beliefs to this ideology.

Only two women, Henrietta Mitchel Martin and Finola, believed in a northern agenda of sorts. This became evident when these two women became involved in the home-rule movement. Henrietta attempted to convert northern Protestants to nationalism; Finola campaigned to improve the lot of the industrial workers.

The activists in the northern movement varied. Jenny Mitchel, Henrietta Mitchel Martin and Margaret Hughes wrote articles for the Young Ireland newspapers. As wives of Young Irelanders, Susan Hughes and Jenny Mitchel gave their husbands much needed support. Jenny became a public figure and raised support for the nationalist cause. Henrietta became a public figure later on in life when she supported her husband in his home-rule endeavours. Finola was a poetess, and she later wrote about the home-rule cause.

Why were these women important to the home-rule cause? As Ulster nationalists they were living examples of Young Ireland's claim that their beliefs embraced all classes and creeds of people. As women they emphasised the importance of women in Young Ireland, and the nationalist movement in general. Their activities showed the diversity of female involvement. It was impossible for any of these women to become nationalist leaders at this time. However, they were all strong, independent characters, and they were not put off by the social restraints placed upon them. They deviated from women's traditional role and also from class restrictions. Generally an association with the Young Ireland group was not seen as acceptable behaviour for upper- and middle-class women, especially after Young Ireland left the Repeal Association in 1846. After this Young Irelanders were seen as extremely dangerous radicals. These women, however, had the courage to become involved in a movement which was often opposed to the beliefs they had been taught at school. Finola, as a Protestant gentlewoman, acted against the political beliefs of her class and community. Others, like Mitchel and Hughes, supported some kind of nationalist tradition, and this may have influenced their decision to take part in the Young Ireland movement.

Nationalism gave women the chance to voice their hopes and beliefs. The emphasis on education and writing in the Young Ireland movement allowed women to participate, and to influence a lot of people through the organisation's newspapers and other publications. Young Ireland's ideology was romantic, but it had an important impact on ideas. The Ulsterwomen contributed to this ideology in their own way. These women were not feminists, and women's issues were not at the forefront of their agenda; however, their example encouraged other women to become involved in politics.

These women were perhaps not typical of Ulsterwomen, but they brought to the Young Ireland movement their independence, coupled with stubbornness, strength, and readiness for action.

Chapter 4

The Ulster Women's Unionist Council

Ferdinand Braudel's term 'submerged history' can be applied to women who, until recently, have been denied a historical role. Placing women at the centre of enquiry poses a serious challenge as the role of the women of Ulster has previously been neglected by historians. To take the late nineteenth century as an example, attention has been mostly focused on the opposed doctrines of Unionism and nationalism. Even here in politics, a male preserve, women were now included, but much research into their role must take place before any theoretical framework can be applied. In the study of women in politics, a wide definition of politics should be adopted.

Politically active women have always constituted a smaller minority of their sex than men, but what prompts women to become active in politics? It is not wise to dismiss any organisation as purely male, though most organisations were controlled by men.

The Ulster Women's Unionist Council (UWUC) was formed on 23 January 1911 with the purpose of supporting male Unionists opposed to home rule in Ireland. The organisation proved to be sufficiently pliable to undertake war work during the First World

War and to adapt to circumstances in the post-war period. The UWUC was a conservative body with few pretensions of influencing policy and with no ambition to disrupt the status quo. The organisation believed that it should be part of a steady, silent movement, but this should not place it within the ranks of the historically insignificant.

In the period just before and during the First World War women became involved in party-political work – not for feminist reasons, but for pragmatic reasons. The Corrupt and Illegal Practices Act of 1883 forbade the payment of political canvassers, and the extension of the electoral franchise in 1884 encouraged party organisers to reconsider their policies. The emergence of women's institutions from the late nineteenth century should be identified with a background of mixed-up party systems. An organisation network now tried to win the energies of party workers, who were to become mainly female. Women became a source of voluntary labour. After 1900 women became more prominent in politics, and they volunteered in their thousands. Although women were excluded from political office until 1918, women's institutions made great contributions to the political process before this date. The UWUC may be placed within this context. In Ulster, women had been involved in the nineteenth-century protests against the introduction of home rule in 1886 and in 1893. The institution of a formal body of women Unionists was brought about by a heightened sense of politics, following the House of Lords' veto of the Parliament Act of 1911.

The UWUC was governed by an executive committee headed by a president. Some of the council's office holders and representatives were members of local Unionist associations. The UWUC met regularly to discuss policies, progress and problems.

The inaugural meeting of the UWUC took place in Belfast in January 1911, and they started work immediately, canvassing voters and helping to bring every single voter to the poll during the election. Most voters in Ulster were in favour of the Union, and the women were behind the men in striving for a noble cause.

The UWUC co-operated with the men's Ulster Unionist Council in promoting religious, economic, constitutional and imperial arguments opposed to home rule. The women proved themselves to be astute; they realised that the case against home rule should be urged mainly on social and economic grounds. The charge of Ulster bigotry should be avoided. For example, Lady Cecil Craig assessed the advantages and disadvantages of home rule when addressing the annual meeting of the East Down Women's Unionist Association in 1914. Apart from their own detestation of the bill in Ulster, it was also bad for the rest of Ireland, the finance being absolutely unsound. There was also no desire for it in the south and west, except among political agitators and ignorant peasants, who were told that once home rule came into effect Ireland would be a land of milk and honey, and such a thing as paying rent would become unknown.

The UWUC also talked about a 'women's dimension' to home rule. In 1911 women's political action was portrayed as an extension of their maternal responsibilities. It was said that each woman should play her part to stem the tide of home rule. The Union meant everything to them – their civil and religious liberty, their homes and children. Once the Union was severed there would be no outlook in Ulster but strife and bitterness. Home was a woman's first consideration. In the event of home rule being passed, the sanctity of home life in Ulster would be violated. The UWUC stressed the point that women and their dependants would eventually suffer most under home rule, for when bad times came, and work was hard to find, women and children were affected more than men.

The UWUC rapidly developed into a strong, dynamic and democratic body. Membership was high. The council was popular and it co-ordinated the activities of the Unionist women. During the first month of its existence over 4,000 women joined the

West Belfast branch. By March 1911, women's Unionist associations affiliated to the UWUC had been formed in Belfast, Londonderry, Antrim, Armagh, Tyrone, Fermanagh and Monaghan. Within a year of its foundation the minutes of the organisation record membership at 40,000. Members were chiefly drawn from the middle and upper classes, and its leaders were almost exclusively upper-class. The 2nd Duchess of Abercorn was president in 1911–13, succeeded by the 6th Marchioness of Londonderry (1913–21) and Lady Cecil Craig (1923–42). In the period 1911–39 only one of the ten vice presidents was untitled. In Ulster and the rest of Ireland, and throughout Britain, women of the upper classes had the time and leisure to carry out public work. However, within the council there was no membership qualification in regard to social background. Undoubtedly some working-class women were involved. For example, it has been alleged that 8 per cent of the West Belfast branch of the council were millworkers and shop girls.

The council appointed a male organising secretary in 1911.

The council seems not to have experienced an initial learning phase; they seem always to have been sure which direction they should take. Four months after the establishment of the council, six of its members were in England canvassing electoral support for a Unionist candidate. By May 1911 the council's executive sent women speakers around Ireland to study the Irish question at first hand. In their canvassing work the UWUC co-operated with the women's pro-Unionist associations in England and Scotland, such as the Primrose League and the Women's Amalgamated Tariff Reform Association.

For the UWUC the Union was paramount and all other matters were of secondary importance. The make-up of the council revealed their political priority: the sole object of the council was to secure the union of Great Britain and Ireland. However, all Unionist activities were stopped to face the third, and most severe, home-rule crisis, in 1912–14.

Edward Carson wrote to Lady Theresa Londonderry in March 1912, and, after saying that this was a very private matter, he told her that he had made up his mind to recommend drastic action in Ulster. He said there was a growing feeling that they did not mean business, but this was a critical year and he was prepared for any risks.

There was a lot of press coverage of public demonstrations organised by the UWUC. The organisation appears to have been valued for its publicity value. L. Cope Cornford, the editor of various Unionist publications, contacted Lady Theresa Londonderry. She said that the press as a whole accepted that the UWUC performed a useful role. It was essential that interest should be maintained, but she foresaw a difficulty there. If the UWUC could issue another manifesto, and take some action, it would help considerably.

The sense of crisis among Unionists helped the UWUC to gain momentum. Attendance figures at female Unionist meetings emphasises the high level of enthusiasm that Unionism could arouse. For example, 10,000 women attended a council demonstration in October 1912. In 1913 they organised a meeting to welcome Edward Carson on his first visit to West Belfast, and this was estimated to be the largest gathering ever to have taken place in Ireland. Attendance was reckoned to be over 25,000.

As well as mass demonstrations, Unionist women also held many drawing-room meetings. For instance, Lady Theresa Londonderry urged women to march with their menfolk to oppose home rule. There was no sacrifice they would not make. They felt that their cause was threatened by the apathy of the people in England towards home rule, so they attempted to overcome this apathy.

The council was involved in comprehensive petitioning. In January 1912 they launched a women's petition against the 'Ne Temere' Papal decree. Within a month this petition was a mile in length, and it eventually boasted 104,301 signatories by the time it was presented to Parliament by Sir John Lonsdale in June 1912. It outlined Unionist women's objections to home rule; it said that serious dangers would arise to challenge their social and domestic liberties. No legislative safeguards would avail to protect them against such dangers.

The Roman Catholic Church refused to recognise the binding effects of any agreements which would threaten its position. It claimed that it should control education and lay down marriage laws. The petition argued that in an Irish parliament the natural instincts of humanity would be of no avail against the dictates of the Church of Rome. The dominating power of ecclesiatics over education in Ireland would be greatly increased. There would be no prospect of beneficial legislation to help with conditions of work for the women, for Irish nationalists strongly opposed such measures in Parliament. No valid reasons had been put forward for depriving Irishwomen of their rights and privileges.

In May 1912 the UWUC collected over 100,000 women's signatures. Another petition against introducing home rule was also forwarded to the House of Commons.

Unionist leaders were aware of the importance of maintaining unity and discipline within their ranks; it was important to present a favourable public image of Ulster Unionism to the English electorate. Many attempts were made to show that Unionists were respectable and had valid reasons for resisting home rule.

A scheme for the establishment of an Ulster covenant was introduced into Parliament, proclaiming Unionist solidarity, self-discipline and determination. Women, however, were barred from signing the male Unionist covenant. The UWUC therefore organised their own declaration with the aim of associating women with the Unionist men of Ulster in their opposition to home rule; 28 September 1912 was designated as the day of the collection of signatures for both the declaration and the covenant – 234,206 men signed the covenant, and 234,046 women signed the declaration.

The UWUC was also responsible for sending thousands of leaflets and newspapers to Britain, America and the empire explaining the Unionist stance against home rule. The UWUC aimed not only to arouse opinion against home rule in Ulster, but also to publicise what Unionists believed to be the true character of Irish nationalists, who, it was said, were not the harmless rabble that Mr Redmond had described. Nationalists painted the future of Ireland in glowing colours, but Protestants did not come into the picture. It was a masterpiece of Impressionist painting, and the further one stood away from it the better it looked.

The women's work was extensive and unrelenting. Working through their belief that prevention was better than a cure, the council established a literary subcommittee to organise their propaganda workload. By September 1913, 10,000 leaflets and newspapers were being sent weekly to Great Britain under the control of the UWUC. Between 13 March and 1 June 1913 information was sent to over 14,000 electors in sixty-five constituencies. Local associations of the UWUC were coupled with English women's Unionist associations. By 1912 twenty-one of thirty-two branches, representing 66 per cent of the UWUC were involved in this work. Many women Unionists were sent to work on the mainland, and by March 1913 nineteen women were permanently based in Britain, working as Unionist 'missionaries'. By the end of that year it was calculated that not less than 100,000 electors heard the Unionist case from the lips of Unionist women. Workers from the UWUC were often requested by other political organisations to spread the home-rule word, which suggests that they were effective propagandists. They were certainly in demand, and in 1912 the council averred that the speakers were most anxious to address undecided audiences rather than meetings of convinced Unionists.

The council's activities were not limited to demonstrations and propaganda in co-operation with the Ulster Unionist Council (UUC). Unionist women made a contribution to the Carson Fund, which had been established in 1912 to oppose home rule. It also worked closely with the Ulster Volunteer Force (UVF), which had been set up to convince people on the mainland of Unionist determination not to accept home rule. The UVF was backed by a strong body of women. The UWUC drafted a scheme for the training of the UVF corps in nursing, driving and signalling. First-aid classes were held, fund-raising was undertaken and supplies for medical units were established throughout Ulster.

Unionists tended to focus solely on their opposition to home rule, but the issue of women's suffrage claimed their attention during the third home-rule crisis. On questions like women's suffrage the women might have held different opinions, but on the question of the Union there were no differences – the union was their rallying point, and this issue held them together with great force. Nevertheless the existence of the council seems to have had a positive impact on the question of women's enfranchisement; by bringing women into the political spotlight and initiating extensive political work among women, the UWUC provided evidence of how women could be visibly active in politics. There were great campaigners within the ranks of the women's council. However, the women's council was unable to evade totally the question of women's suffrage. A suffragette movement had begun in Ulster in 1913, and many women Unionists wanted to establish a provisional government in Ulster that would include women.

Carson, an opponent of women's suffrage, concentrated upon divisions within his own party.

The UWUC was also concerned about the political nature of demands for women's suffrage. In September 1913 Lady Dufferin wrote to Lady Londonderry in connection with the Unionist plan to include women in the provisional government. There was a great deal of feeling about this. The suffragettes were triumphant, but others had written to say that they would veto the resolution. She came to the conclusion that it would be best to ignore the part of the letter dealing with suffrage – the UWUC stood solely for the establishment of home rule. On other questions they might be divided, so it was important that they refrain from any expression of opinion on other issues. She realised that in any discussion of home rule there would be unpleasantness.

This reluctance to discuss the question of women's enfranchisement continued. In March 1914, the UWUC president, Lady Londonderry, asked that the organisation should take action in connection with the recent deputation of suffragettes to Sir Edward Carson. It was advised not to reopen the matter. The UWUC made no further comment on suffrage, but instead stepped up their political activities. By July 1914 Unionists saw civil war as their only choice, but the UWUC were appalled by this prospect. They were, however, determined to continue to support the male Unionists. They said that they must be prepared for the worst, and they would stand with their men to the last. To the women the very thought of strife and bloodshed was horrific; in such times it was women that suffered most, but the women of Ulster were resolved to be a help, rather than a hindrance, to the men. They were resolved to give them sympathy, encouragement, approval and admiration.

The situation was radically altered with the outbreak of the First World War in August 1914. This led to a cessation of suffragette militancy and Unionist plans for civil war. The conflict moved from Ulster to the wider field of Europe.

The entire Unionist campaign was officially suspended for the length of the war. However, where activities proved to be dangerous to the Unionist cause, the UWUC did embark upon political activity. The organisation of the UWUC remained operative, but their priorities altered. With the outbreak of war the council believed that it was its duty to see that the families of servicemen were cared for, and that any want and suffering that might result would be minimised. To reach this target the women's council became engaged in much charity work, working alongside organisations like the Soldiers' and Sailors' Families Association.

Only three months after the outbreak of the war, Unionist women discussed equipping the Ulster Division with comforts, and they offered £100 towards the purchase of a machine gun or, failing that, an ambulance. Pacifist beliefs had no place within their wartime rhetoric. It seems likely that the purchase of a machine gun provided a way for women to become indirectly involved in the male preserve of fighting. In the end, the council bought an ambulance, and it was used in France during the war.

In August 1914 the UWUC inaugurated the Ulster Women's Gift Fund for soldiers, and by 1918 it had raised in excess of £100,000. Unionist headquarters in Belfast were converted into premises where the women met and packed and dispatched food. They also provided military dressings not only for Irish regiments, but for other army and naval contingents and hospitals. In 1916 this work was augmented by a fund to provide similar comforts for prisoners of war. Visits to families of men serving in the war were also organised, and the council made arrangements to care for those who were discharged from the forces on medical grounds. UVF hospitals in Belfast and France received the special attention of the council; for instance, they financed the running of the French UVF hospital in 1914–16.

The war was being fought on an international scale, but Ulster was still the focus of the UWUC.

Unionist women were also involved in recruiting Voluntary Aid Detachments and soldiers for both the Ulster and imperial forces, but they only undertook to do this work after firm assurances had been received in regard to their own position.

Feminism in the ranks of women's Unionism was usually overridden by political concerns, though there was still some importance attached to women's rights. The UWUC also protested against the exclusion of Ireland from the Compulsory

Military Service Acts of 1916 and 1918. In 1916 they declared that members of the UWUC represented a quarter of a million loyal women in the province. They protested against the refusal of the government to unite people with their fellow citizens in Great Britain in a bond of common service for the Empire.

The formal Unionist political work was suspended, and the council was concerned with its own domestic position, for there was a sense of insecurity. The women remained home in Ulster and had difficulty in overlooking the uncertainty of their own position; they continued to question how the post-war situation would affect them. In 1916 the council altered its constitution to meet the demands of war. The UWUC undertook political work through its individual members rather than through its general network. For example, in 1917 the council urged that its members should try to reach as many colonial soldiers as possible and to instruct them on home-rule matters. The council was worried about the outcome of a post-war general election. They worked continually to keep the electoral registers up-to-date. This work became important after the granting of the franchise to women aged thirty or over in February 1918.

The Redistribution of Seats (Ireland) Act in the same year made it necessary to reorganise several existing branches of the UWUC and to establish branches in newly created electoral areas. This was political work that the council refused to disregard. By June 1918, the UWUC reaffirmed their objective to be entirely occupied in planning a scheme to defeat the latest home-rule measure. War-weariness was a problem, and the political situation was changing. The UWUC had become increasingly discontent with Unionist leaders, who were now openly discouraging the UWUC from undertaking widespread political work. Their disapproval was loudly expressed when they demanded a definition of their status in June 1918, particularly in regard to the Unionist Party. The UWUC proclaimed that during the last four years their opinion on any political matter had never been sought. They themselves had been silent in the face of a slow disintegration of power. Their advice had never been asked when the covenant was broken. No intimation had been given about the suggested federal system. Nevertheless they held fast to their Unionist opinions; their voice was heard and acted upon – though perhaps the Ulster Unionist Council thought of them as an entirely negligible quantity. There was no attempt to emphasise any difference between the men and women of Ulster. The feeling was that they should be comrades in arms in defence of a common cause.

What was the position of the UWUC? Was it right and just that they should be in this position? Were they wise in spending large sums of money, troubling themselves and expending their health and strength? They could not give up their position as the leading women's association in Ulster, for there were many anxieties and dangers that had to be faced in regard to the position of women in society. If anything, they needed more power for immediate action. They had struggled to keep their people together, to educate women, and to bring the war to a satisfactory conclusion. They now had to stand up for the rights of Ulsterwomen. They resolved to fight under the motto 'Union Is Strength'.

This proved to be the signal for change. Unionist leaders gave the women's council permission to reorganise and to exist as a separate organisation. In 1918, women were granted twelve separate representatives on the UUC. A joint committee of the men's and women's councils was established to co-ordinate consultation and co-operation between the two movements.

During the post-war period the political world of the women's council was fully revived, and they spread their area of interest. Preceding the establishment of the Ulster Parliament, the Unionists accepted six-county exclusion for Ulster, and not the nine counties that had been originally suggested.

Partition was a thorn in the side of the UWUC, even during

the First World War. Lady Dufferin expressed the organisation's anxiety. Writing to Lady Londonderry in July 1916, she said that their women were naturally upset with the turn of events and were longing to get into action. They were heartbroken over the possible partition of Ulster, and were still hoping some better solution to their difficulties might transpire.

Edith Mercier Clement voiced similar sentiments to the council's president. She said they should hold together with supporters in the three other counties of Ulster, but many of them were too sad to even want to attend the committee. It was essential, she said, to show them that they meant more to us than ever before because of the sacrifices they had made. It is hard to form any idea of why so many women were not open to compromise. They should not have consented to anything that meant the breaking of the covenant.

In April 1919 Lady Cecil Craig expressed sentiments that summarised the Unionist women's position on partition. They all agreed that they would remain under the Union; but if this was not possible, they would try their best. Partition was debated at a UWUC meeting in March 1920, where the majority agreed that Ulster should remain intact to uphold the covenant. The council sent representatives to the UUC meeting held to decide a geographical definition of Ulster, but the UWUC imposed no restrictions on their representatives. They were left free to vote as their consciences directed them. At length the UWUC decided upon six-county exclusion, but there was some internal dissent and resignations occurred within their ranks.

The establishment of a form of government which was entirely unasked for by the majority of people in Ulster ensured the continuation of the work of the UWUC. It was said that the future held much uncertainty for the loyal population of the Six Counties. Their watchword was still 'Union'. Their struggle against enemies of the British Empire had been transferred to a new field. Ulster stood alone as she had never done before, and every loyal Ulsterwoman was urged to realise her responsibilities. By working and voting, women could hold fast to civil rights and religious liberty, which had been handed down to them as a sacred trust.

By 1927 the UWUC was stressing the importance of resisting any false sense of political security and of maintaining their organisation at the highest degree of perfection. If crisis should again arise, the loyal women of Ulster should be prepared. With this end in view, they resolved that the necessary machinery would be kept in running order.

Running alongside the political insecurity was the question of women's votes. The UWUC's attitude to the partial enfranchisement of women in 1918 was complex. It reveals much, both about their war policy and about the attitude of the UUC towards women in politics. The UWUC tried to ensure that every Ulsterwoman who was entitled to vote was on the electoral register. The Duchess of Abercorn, addressing a women's Unionist demonstration in Belfast in May 1921 said that the women had never clamoured to vote, but now they had got the vote she was confident they would use it for the safety, honour and welfare of their churches, their country, their homes and their children by helping to put a strong government in power. She said that no personal feeling should prevent women from voting, no matter what might be the claims of children, home or business.

The organisation, however, was conservative. It was coupled with the prevalent insecurity concerning the establishment of a separate legislature for Northern Ireland, and the UWUC seems to have been dissuaded from patronising female parliamentary candidates. In 1921 they expressed their view that the time was not ripe for this, and that the essential thing in the first parliament was to preserve the Unionist cause. Too much organisation and construction work would be necessary, for which the women would not have the necessary experience. On the whole men candidates were preferred. Male Unionist leaders encouraged women to use their vote for the Unionist cause. James Craig said that since they had obtained the vote it was up to women to use their influence in every possible way for raising the hearts of the masses and looking after their welfare, and to take an interest in the vast fields that lay before them in making Ulster a better place for both men and women to live in. This was a task that was as much a woman's as it was a man's.

Sir Edward Carson addressed the UWUC in February 1921 at the annual general meeting. He emphasised the responsibilities of women as a result of the franchise. He assisted them in choosing candidates that would be representative of their views. James Craig put forward similar views. A hard campaign lay before them, the success of which would depend upon the women of Ulster. Before any woman put herself forward for Parliament, he said, she should fully considered the matter. 'Patience' should be the watchword of the moment.

The Unionists had an electoral victory in 1921, and Craig paid tribute to his supporters. He stated that he was the proudest of men.

The council essentially sacrificed feminist beliefs for the ultimate benefit of the province. The UWUC had a considerable store of political and organisational experience, but they had a lack of confidence in their women. The men reduced the women to a secondary status.

Throughout the 1920s the UWUC worked to maximise the possibility of Unionist candidates being elected, but they never encouraged women candidates to come forward and stand in elections.

The council's attitude towards women standing for election to less important bodies than the imperial Parliament was more progressive. For example, in March 1919 they openly encouraged all their branches to select suitable females for urban and district county councils. From March 1920 women Unionist candidates, standing in the Poor Law elections for the boards of guardians, received official and financial support from the council, and by 1930 they declared that Poor Law work was women's work.

The UWUC also encouraged women's political participation in other ways. During the interwar years they funded scholarships to train Unionist women in politics, economics and citizenship. They employed female trainee political organisers in their headquarters. Following the further extension of the vote to those over twenty-one in 1928, the UWUC considered it essential that women Unionists should remain fully organised to assert their rights, but no overt encouragement was ever given to women standing for parliamentary elections during the period 1918–40.

Between the wars the council did not rest from work. During 1930 over 7,000 propaganda leaflets were sent under their auspices. Their speakers addressed over 160 meetings. Three new associations and twenty-nine new branches of the council were formed.

Educational propaganda remained the focus of their work. In 1934 they reported a steady advance being made along the lines of political education. The goal was that every woman voter should be given a chance of studying Unionist aims and ideals, so the Unionist women of Ulster realised their political responsibilities and their power as citizens.

The council also expanded its objectives, making Unionism appear relevant to Ulster's interwar position. The women further organised and continued their public activities. They campaigned against Sinn Fein activity in Britain, America and the Dominions. They opposed socialism and the rise of sectarian violence in Ulster. They also replied to press statements that gave what Unionists considered to be false information on the Irish question. Unionist women also promoted the buying of empire-produced goods and the enforcement of licensing legislation. Demonstrations and petitioning remained a feature of their work.

Clubs for girls were established to recruit future women voters to Unionism. Public-speaking competitions and classes were held, and a speakers class for men was also established.

In the interwar period there was also evidence of increasing levels of co-operation between the UWUC and their male counterparts. This was perhaps because of women's enfranchisement. From 1924 to 1926 both councils appointed male and female travelling organisers. On many occasions the UUC provided free literature for the UWUC. The two bodies of popular Unionism co-operated in establishing branches of the Junior Imperial League in Ulster to educate the young, and they jointly raised funds to erect Carson's memorial stone in Belfast Cathedral.

It has been claimed that the UWUC was a non-sectarian body, but their bestowal of representatives to the Women's Loyal Orange Lodges in 1920 reflects an overlap of personnel between the two bodies. As well as this the UWUC distributed 10,000 leaflets pointing out the eviction of Protestants from Catholic areas of Belfast. In 1932 they discussed whether any steps had been taken to prevent the penetration of Roman Catholics into certain parts of Ulster, and if anything could be done to prevent enemies of loyalism buying property over the heads of Protestants.

War had perhaps changed the attitude to women in society, but it failed to permanently alter the belief that women were responsible for the home life of the nation. The art of the housewife is a science requiring dedication. Women were required to take a keen interest in their homes, and to take seriously their duties. Women believed that if they had safe and happy homes in which they could raise their children, they would nurture a race of men who would rally to the needs of their country in its extreme hour. It was the men that won the war, but it was the women that would win the peace.

Such sentiments were amply expressed in the papers that the UWUC produced between the wars. Their first paper, entitled

Ulsterwoman: A Journal for Union and Progress, was published from July 1919 until August 1920. Its successor, *Northern Ireland, Home and Politics: A Journal for Women*, was published from October 1925 to June 1927. The council's president at this time, the 3rd Duchess of Abercorn, stated that the aim of the paper was to bring before Ulsterwomen the main questions of the day in a way that would not make too great a demand on the busy women's time. Ulsterwomen had always been interested in politics, but they could do more. They should be able to give a reason for their beliefs and reply to those that try to refute them. Every woman had the Unionist cause at heart, and the UWUC was anxious about involving workers in town and country in questions about housing, education or reconstruction schemes. They did, however, take advantage of the opportunities that the journal afforded.

Sir Edward Carson wrote an article in the first edition of the journal. In it he praised the work of female Unionists, but his tone was that of talking down. He gave his best wishes to the paper. *Ulsterwoman*'s contents were a bit contradictory. Articles discussing women's positions in trade unions appeared alongside articles praising the role of women during the war. Gardening and other activities were also seen as suitable for women's attention.

Northern Ireland, Home and Politics: A Journal for Women is quite a revealing title – putting home before politics. The paper concentrated on issues like the boundary question, along with articles on wider issues like unemployment, women's pensions, the empire and socialism as well as areas which seem more typically women's territory. A report from a Unionist and conservative women's conference reveals little or no feminism in their discussions, but only a desire to discover what was best for Ireland. The Foreign Secretary paid the women Unionists a compliment by addressing them as though they were men.

Women's social responsibilities were also discussed in the

journal. For example, in April 1927, Dehra Chichester, one of the first women MPs for Northern Ireland, wrote an article assuring women that participation in government was not incompatible with women's social role. Women's advent into branches of public life did not necessarily mean the end of home life. It was possible for them to combine public and private duties. Local government work could be entirely interwoven with the root and fibre of home life.

One of the journal's most overtly feminist articles was published anonymously in August 1926. It said that undoubtedly women had been influential in Ulster from earliest times. It was only about fifteen years ago, the article said, that women began to knock more determinedly at the doors which men had held closed, and to demand admission. A stern negative was usually returned. At length came the war, and at once the closed doors fell down like the walls of Jericho. The UWUC could, if it wanted, shape the political destiny of Northern Ireland.

In spite of this strange feminism, the UWUC conception of the womanly ideal persisted throughout the interwar years. Even though the organisation knew from its own experience that women could organise into an effective force, they did not want to assert their political rights too firmly. This might mean loss of favour with male Unionists. *Ulsterwoman* was cautious not to suggest that the men had failed in their efforts on behalf of the Union. There was a part of the question that they did not touch, and aspects of it that appealed more to women than to men.

Members of the council felt that the time had come when they should play their part independently. They realised that there were great moral and social issues at stake – questions of housing, home and family that depended upon the Union. Only women could understand these issues. The question of class were secondary to the issues of home and happiness. They believed that everyone should have the right to live under conditions that would make for the greatest happiness for the greatest number.

The council therefore assumed an ambiguous position. The fusion of conservatism and feminism reflects the interwar experience of British women. It appears that the vote and extensive war work had not made much impact on women's social status. It had, however, increased their hopes. For many women, the interwar period was a period of uncertainty with regard to feminist activity. Women were treated as a form of surplus population. Now that the men had returned from the war they had been forced out of the workplace and back into their homes.

Their reluctance to stand in Parliamentary elections was not restricted to Ulster. The interwar experience of the UWUC largely conforms to that on the British mainland.

The council succeeded in encouraging interest and support for the advancement of women whilst preserving Unionist principles. In some ways they took one feminist step forward and two conservative steps back.

The UWUC again set politics aside throughout the Second World War to concentrate on war work. This decision was more determined than it had been two decades before in the First World War. As in the previous conflict, women's war effort provided no guarantee of change. Lady Edith Londonderry recorded in her biography that it was unjust to say that women as a whole had a very poor time indeed during these years. The Second World War produced an even greater materialism, fuelled by pro-nationalist interests. There was only a slight blurring of sexual divisions; attitudes were left largely unchanged.

The period 1911 to 1940 saw dramatic legislative and social changes in Britain. By the late 1930s women possessed full property, political and judicial rights, but there was no progressive erosion of the distinction between what were deemed to be feminine and masculine spheres. By 1909 it was believed that women's enfranchisement would produce a great revolution of boundless significance that would worry England. It was thought that women's suffrage would rapidly lead to its logical conclusion – the complete equality of men and women.

The result proved to be different. Women emerged as a political force, but the UWUC also inspired in many women a sense of freedom and independence that was unavailable to women in other spheres. This was particularly so for their middle-class members, who were more firmly entrenched in the domestic front than their upper-class or working-class sisters. The council must be viewed as a women's organisation mostly under male control. The UWUC contributed to the strength of popular Unionism, but the council proved to be more flexible in the interwar years than many of its counterparts. It continued to introduce women into the movement and to take an active role in politics.

The history of the UWUC reveals that Ulster Unionism was not only a male preserve, yet in many accounts their role is not acknowledged. For example, Ronald McNeill, author of the 1922 publication *Ulster's Stand for Union*, painted women as being idle sightseers, not a genuine political force. They were, however, scarcely less active than men as far as organisation was concerned. When hard times for the Union came there was no apathy among Ulster's Protestant women. They very quickly became an effective force – just as effective as the men.

The UWUC developed from a political auxiliary force opposed to home rule out of a deep-seated sense of duty. When the achievements of the UWUC are considered, Unionism is exposed as a political belief which cuts across the gender divide. The organisation, having thousands of members, demanded recognition. Dedicated women passed from household duties into Ulster's politics. They made a valuable contribution to the Unionist cause.

Chapter 5

The Ulster Revival

The Ulster Revival of 1859 came suddenly. It took place mainly in the Protestant communities of Antrim and Down, and to a lesser extent in counties Londonderry, Tyrone and Armagh. Members of the Anglican established church, Methodists and Baptists participated in the movement, but the majority of those involved were Presbyterians, simply because they formed the largest part of the Protestant community. In the mainly Catholic counties of Donegal, Cavan and Monaghan the revival had lesser success.

A revival is essentially an increase in interest in religion, and it manifests itself in great numbers of conversions over a short period of time. It is characterised by the occurrence of Pentecostal phenomena, a high level of lay enthusiasm, and the moral transformation of society.

This is what undoubtedly happened in Ulster. During the summer, various types of religious meetings were held at frequent intervals and in numerous locations. People were exhorted to forsake their sins and turn to Christ – a process of sudden change that involved intense feelings of agony and guilt and eventual belief. The intensity of these crowded meetings caused many men to react to their spiritual anguish in physical ways – from moaning and sobbing to fits of shaking, visions and trances. The appearance of stigma-like markings was not unknown. The laity fell under the leadership of clergymen, conducting prayer meetings, assisting with conversions and preaching in public. Religious leaders concentrated on the revival's more pragmatic goals of church development.

The inevitable result was a moral transformation of society. The new converts forsook their old ways, renouncing violence, drunkenness, prostitution, family strife, laziness, vulgarity, Sabbath-breaking and other vices.

Women featured in many reports that were published in 1859 and 1860, and what these women said was recorded by a male reporter or clergyman. This creates certain difficulties of interpretation, but it is still possible to obtain a sense of what women believed and what motivated them to embrace religion. The explanation appears to be simple: women were drawn to religion for practical, down-to-earth reasons.

According to the census of 1851 the population of Ulster was 2,011,880. The overall population of the province had declined, but the population of Belfast was rapidly increasing. It was just over 100,000 in 1851, rising to just over 121,000 a decade later – an increase of about 15 per cent. In Belfast in 1851 about 53 per cent of the adult population were women; in 1861 it had risen to 54 per cent – perhaps as a result of the increasing numbers of jobs available for women in the linen industry.

It appears that the majority of women involved in the revival were from the lower classes. In the country they were farmers' or labourers' wives, daughters and servants; in Belfast they were millworkers or occupied in some other branch of the textile industry – weaving, shirt-making or undertaking sewn-muslin work. Other occupations included shopkeepers, washerwomen, street sellers, domestic servants and prostitutes. Some middle-class women attended these meetings, but, despite claims that the revival reached all classes of the population, it was mainly labouring women that were involved.

Much life in nineteenth-century Ulster reflected the concept of 'separate spheres'. Activities, responsibilities, duties and behaviour could be labelled as belonging to either the female or the male sphere. Women had an important role in religion, for they were expected to exert a moral influence upon society and their families. They were judged to be open to religious experience, and they were considered responsible for the maintenance of a Christian atmosphere in the home. The Methodist Conference, in its annual address to its members in 1859, stressed the important role of women; Methodism depended upon mothers and upon elder sisters to uphold the word.

The Ulster Revival provides an ideal context in which to examine the responsibilities of women within the family, and the conflicting demands that their roles demanded. On the one hand women were said to be sympathetic, virtuous and sensitive to religious feeling – so they should set an example for men, who were easily open to moral corruption – but they were also considered to be nervous, excitable, weak, and prone to fits, visions and physical manifestations. There was the stereotype of women praying to God for help, devout in every respect. As a result, many believe that the conversion made female souls delightful to watch – their faces glowed.

Conversion was also accompanied by great enthusiasm for praying. According to the Reverend Samuel J. Moore, women prayed with sweet, referential familiarity. When the Reverend Moore tried to pray with a female convert he was forced to stop because her prayer was much more eloquent than his.

Society already considered women as virtuous and religious; the revival highlighted these qualities to a supernatural level. For those women outside the female stereotype, such as working women and prostitutes, the revival restored them to respectability. Even though they might have been previously coarse, the process of conversion could bless them with an exceptional ability to pray. Every movement, every gesture of the person – of the face, the head, the hands – would become the very perfection of gracefulness, even though the woman might be uneducated and previously uncouth and awkward.

Prostitutes presented the most blatant violation of this feminine ideal, and they were considered to be the worst examples of depraved womanhood by the faithful. The very nature of their profession had deprived them of their feminine virtue, and they had sunk to the lowest level of society. As a consequence the conversion of prostitutes functioned as a powerful endorsement of revivalism. The *Londonderry Guardian*, for example, claimed that, by means of the many revival meetings held throughout the city, eight prostitutes had seen the light, showing that good was produced even amongst the most abandoned of classes. The conversion of these immoral women was seen as proof that the revival was a work of God. Only by supernatural means, it was thought, could this transformation have occurred. One former prostitute was quoted as saying that for eleven years she had been a prostitute on the streets of Portadown, and no beast could have lived a more filthy life than she did. Now Jesus had found her and brought her to Himself. She said she would gladly work her fingers to the bone rather than leave Him again.

Even when women were below the established feminine ideal, as a result of conversion and revival there was hope for her.

Grace, virtue and holiness were deemed essential to the female role in society, and contemporaries viewed the revival as restoring women to their proper place, making working women respectable by the divine word of God. For those women that were already respectable, the revival helped to underline the view that their religious and moral influence was a duty.

In contrast, a writer for the *Northern Standard* expressed his surprise that no fervour had been shown at a revival meeting at the Presbyterian church in Monaghan, not even after two hours of preaching, not even amongst the excitable female quarter of the congregation. If anyone was going to give in to the revival excitement, popular opinion said that it would be women. Critics of the revival said that stuffy meetings in crowded churches went on until the early hours of the morning, providing opportunities for promiscuous behaviour. They said that the meetings were a forum of disgraceful exhibitions, making women forget their modest role in society. This sort of criticism was reserved for physical manifestations themselves, partly because they occurred more frequently in women.

One of the first recorded cases took place in a Presbyterian church in the Ballymena area. During the course of the meeting a middle-aged married woman from Laymore, County Antrim, appeared to have succumbed to the excitement. She appeared also to be feverish. Her pulse was quick. There was a mark upon her cheeks, her eyes were partly closed and bloodshot, and her face was full of perspiration. Her appetite was bad – she did not eat for fifty-six hours, and she was unable to drink anything but water. After the first four hours of terrible pain and great cries for mercy, she became more composed, but she remained prostrate for nearly three days.

Such behaviour became commonplace throughout Ulster. Women rarely expressed any fear or dread of these great spiritual events; on the contrary, they were often desired as proof of conversion. The clergy soon condemned this attitude and criticised the manifestations as a bodily disease that, if encouraged, became a positive outrage. The behaviour was, some said, against women's nature and almost certain to lead to serious consequences. What those consequences were was left to the imagination. Women were considered more prone to physical manifestations since they were by nature more weak and excitable than men.

The arguments raised over the propriety of physical manifestations raged over and above arguments about the ruination of female virtue. Critics also feared for the mental stability of society, saying that the revival had driven many people insane. There were claims that the mental instability of the population had led to an increase of drunkenness and crime. Preachers worried that the proliferation of lay ministries posed a threat to clerical authority. Supporters of the revival and its critics were united in their confusion surrounding physical excitement. These phenomena were outside their experience. Their ignorance was reflected in their conflicting responses. Ministers that supported the revival attributed the intense feelings to the Holy Spirit.

Though some converted women were transformed into virtuous and pious people by the revival, the physical excitement displayed by some women provided fuel for those who were critical of the movement. As a result of religious fervour these women were stricken down, but women also had the potential to be elevated to a higher religious plane by the revival.

These observations give a good idea of the male attitude to female religious experiences. It is possible, by using accounts in the local newspapers and pamphlets, to gain some idea of how women regarded their own experiences.

Conversion was a central feature of the revival. The first step involved a great consciousness of sin, and the conviction that their sins made them unworthy of Christ; they would go to hell. Women were frequently described expressing words of despair like "I am lost, I am lost", "Lost, O God!" or "I am a godforsaken sinner". Hell was ready for them, and their wickedness was too great to be pardoned. They could not pray. Women commonly visualised this mental struggle with sin as a supernatural battle between Christ and the Devil. Satan sought to drag them from the narrow path they had chosen, but Christ would come to break the Devil's grasp and set them firmly upon the Holy Rock on their journey to heaven. Women had no difficulty in believing that the spiritual realm was able to influence events in the natural world. The realisation of their unworthiness seemed to mean that hell was the only option. This created great despair and agony, which was often expressed in great cries, and even physical self-harm.

Almost as a last hope, Christ was petitioned to save the women from Satan, from hell and from herself. Once she reached a certain point, Jesus stepped in and saved her, he calmed her fears, removed her doubts and gave her the assurance that he had pardoned all her sins. The women often described Christ as wearing a crown of dazzling brightness with a beautiful look on His face. He also became the object of an affection that, although sentimentalised, had sexual overtones. One convert claimed that even maternal love was pale in comparison to her love of Jesus.

Assurance of salvation was one doctrine that women especially clung to. One Agnes J., a factory worker, was under conviction for nearly three weeks when she was assured that God never commenced His work in a soul unless He wanted to save it. She was stricken down. She said her heart felt as if it might burst, but now the burden of sin was gone and her sins had been forgiven. She was full of gratitude, humbled to the ground by the thought of her past sins and neglect of Christ, but now she blessed His name and the Holy Spirit; all was now different. "Never, O never!" she exclaimed, should she doubt He would never let her go.

Accounts such as these could be accompanied by lofty theories that economic change and insecurity were the causes – a desire for reassurance. It could be explained that there was merely a desire to be accepted as an individual and freed from the peril of rejection. Perhaps the changing economic situation increased the need for reassurance. But the women of the time did not view it in these terms. During the Ulster Revival, conversion (and the happiness it provided) was considered from an entirely spiritual perspective.

The way in which women became involved in the conversion

process reveals a great deal about their religious beliefs. Most women were converted as a result of some form of religious group or female support group. A good example of this was the Belfast linen industry. Mill girls, as female workers in the linen mills were known, had a reputation for being reckless and degraded and for possessing an altogether low character. They were often considered to be without spiritual beliefs. The poor reputation of mill girls was partly because of the nature of the work. The prejudices of other working women created a strong group solidarity amongst the mill girls, and this was revealed when the revival passed their way. If one worker was stricken down, it was not uncommon for her friends and for other workers to have a similar experience.

At Davidson's at Ballymena, it was reported that six or seven women were condemned for sin at the beginning of the day. Within one hour, between twenty and thirty women were prostrated, and the mill had to close down for lack of workers.

Another common means of conversion was attendance at the revival activities, including prayer meetings, Bible classes and open-air services. Here women were embraced by their friends of the same sex. If one woman was prostrated under the influence of Jesus, there were likely to be many of her friends in attendance, praying and singing over her. She was then encouraged to discover true salvation.

Clerical restrictions on female teachers encouraged women to form all-female Bible classes. These proved interesting arenas for subsequent conversion.

One girl, the daughter of a tradesman, was saved at a meeting of the Reverend Hugh Hanna. A female friend had been invited to attend a Bible class for girls on the street. Here penmanship, arithmetic and domestic skills were taught.

The influence of family and friends was of the utmost importance apart from the support groups. Women encouraged each other to attend meetings and pray for their unconverted relatives and neighbours. When they visited these under conviction they spoke reassuringly, quoted Scripture, sang hymns and prayed.

The Reverend James Morgan of Fisherwick Presbyterian Church, Belfast, recalled his first revival conversion. She was a poor widow who had doubts about her spiritual condition, and she wanted him to pray for her and give her advice. He gave her the best counsel that he could. He concentrated upon reassuring her that the blood of Jesus would cleanse all of them from all sin. This appeared to quiet her fears somewhat. It was not until she had talked with her maidservant that she became full of joy and peace in believing. She found it reassuring to discuss her sins with friends of the same sex, and this created an atmosphere more conducive of conversion than the doctrinal demands of her minister. Female support groups, be they formal or informal, served as a powerful force for conversion.

Some women claimed to have visions; some were prostrated or fell down into trances that lasted for days; some claimed to be clairvoyant; and some came out in marks which Jesus had placed upon their bodies. Some visions were seen on a corporate level within a given congregation. A few men also came forward, claiming that they had received a direct revelation from their Maker, but these so-called aberrations were an almost entirely female phenomenon. They were widely condemned, even by supporters of the revival.

Determining the truth of these revelations dominated the contemporary debate. Were these events evidence of the Divine or the work of the Devil? Although examination of the visions experienced by women revealed certain truths about how they regarded Christianity and why they built Christ around their lives, many of the clergy did not believe these events were caused by God.

Church attendance was a religious duty, but also a social one, and the wearing of good clothes was considered to be essential.

If the poor did not have the right clothes, they simply did not attend church. Even if the ministers frowned upon this attitude, it was strongly reinforced by the devout. The Reverend Edward Stopford tells the story of one woman who had not been to church for nine years, claiming as an excuse her poor attire. She had been newly converted but still refused to attend church. When Stopford criticised her and encouraged her to attend, the woman replied that it would be easy before God but not so easy before man; she flatly refused.

Cultural concerns about the opinions of others proved to be powerful forces preventing people from taking full advantage of the religious opportunities before them. Some ministers held services in shops and barns so that the poor might be more comfortable in their working clothes.

Women often dreamed of heaven as a place where they would wear beautiful clothes. The woman the Reverend Stopford referred to had a dream in which she saw heaven and Jesus. She said that He looked beautiful, and the angels were worshipping Him as He came towards her. He had something in his hand – it was a gown, and how beautiful it was! It was a Gown of Glory, and it was meant for her. Jesus came straight towards her and put the gown on her Himself. She sat on the throne of God, and Jesus sat beside her.

For this woman, the dress may have represented the wealth she might obtain in this world. Sitting beside Christ on the throne symbolised the social position she lacked.

A woman called Jane, from Belfast, had a similar vision in which the Lord approached her. He brought in his hand a suit, which she said was the Robe of Righteousness. He turned and left her alone.

A Gown of Glory and the Robe of Righteousness suggest that the women hoped for righteousness and status. It was a feature of these robes that there was an emphasis upon beauty, cleanliness and purity. Jesus was many times described as beautiful – part of his beauty being his cleanliness, reflected in the use of terms like *white, clean* and *pure*. Jesus wore white robes, and the path to heaven was white, as was the light that illuminated it. The conversion process was itself a process of becoming spiritually clean.

One woman exclaimed, "O blessed Jesus, come. You are my hope, my life, my all; wash me in Thy most precious blood; take away my filthy garment and cover me in Your own great righteousness."

It was a woman's fate to be dirty, poor and downtrodden; religion provided an alternative vision.

Several of the visions exhibited a more literary flavour. The woman from Laymore, referred to earlier, described a vision in which a Bible was opened before her. She could not read, but a spiritual power endowed her with the ability to understand the Book. She was able to quote at length from the Old and New Testaments and to use them in connection with various prayers and hymns that she uttered. When she was restored to good health this ability faded.

Sometimes the acquisition of new abilities went beyond a dream. Some women showed the ability to read, even though they had been illiterate.

A woman called Mary was illiterate, but whilst in a trance she held the New Testament and tried to look for verses that were relevant for her. She marked the pages by turning down the corners. When she recovered from the trance she had no memory of her experiences, just a feeling of peace.

This striving after peace was part of a general longing for education, secular or spiritual. Sermons could be complex treatises on dogmatic issues, usually lasting over an hour. Women were more than just passive listeners.

Grace Hunter, a Methodist from County Down, was remembered for the intensity with which she listened to the sermons, following the preachers' words closely and taking a lot of notes. Sometimes she confronted preachers on points of doctrine she felt were being neglected, and encouraged them to speak on these subjects more often.

One woman, upon hearing the gospel for the first time, exclaimed to the minister, "Thank God for the meeting!" She thought that God was speaking to her, and she said she could have risen through the ceiling with joy.

What made religious instruction so popular was the fact that it could satisfy the desire for education within a religious context without fear of disapproval. Women may have been encouraged to pursue godly goals as part of their duty as females. In such a way was it possible for women to achieve some degree of self-improvement.

The local church not only functioned as a legitimate sphere of learning, but it also provided one of the few opportunities women had to obtain an informal education. Sunday sermons were the most obvious means, but other options included the many Bible classes, Sunday schools and day schools. Sunday schools offered religious instruction, but also taught basic literacy. Their main function was to teach children, but during the revival they also provided adult instruction. Members of exclusively female classes often gave credit to their local church, which managed the schools, for teaching them how to read. Berry Street Presbyterian Church, Belfast, had the most extensive Sunday-school system. One school, situated on Ewart's Row, educated many millworkers and their families. One student recalled that they had learned to read the Scriptures and the Shorter Catechism. They could write and calculate basic sums.

Methodists supplemented their Sunday schools with class meetings. Teachers were asked to bring new students to these meetings, to introduce them to the procedure and to make them feel welcome. Students provided mutual encouragement. The Methodists saw these meetings as complementary to the Sunday schools.

Working-class men and women enthusiastically sought education of any type or quality. For women, religion provided a legitimate forum for learning, and the churches placed this kind of learning within easy reach. The contents of women's visions reveal this longing for education, but some women were only able to read under supernatural conditions; they lost this ability once they came out of the trance or shortly thereafter. This suggests that illiterate women (among the working classes at least) were considered an anomaly, acceptable only in special situations. Some schools only allowed the Scriptures to be read, and this suggests that clergymen and lay readers hoped to confine women's education strictly to a religious context.

Life in the mid-nineteenth century was quite dangerous. Cholera, factory accidents and shipwrecks occurred frequently and were a constant worry. The visions that the women had during the revival indicate the nearness of death and how they came to terms with it.

There were women who, during their trances, claimed to converse with loved ones who had died. One eight-year-old girl, described as shy, intelligent and well versed in religion, was suddenly prostrated while getting ready for school. She remained in a trance for about five hours, at which point she sat up and cried out that she had been in the company of superhuman beings – much to the surprise of her parents. She affirmed that in her vision she had recognised her infant brother, who had died eleven months after his birth, when she was five years old.

A woman called Mary Sarah Buchanan was in the Kilwarlin Moravian Church in September 1859 when she had a vision. She professed to see those that had died, including the Reverend Zula (the former minister) and his wife.

Critics of the visions called them mere hallucinations, and others went so far as to claim they were the Devil's work. They claimed their occurrence was due to the weak character of the women involved. The validity of these visions remains in question.

The revival was a time of great emotional upset, when people were called upon to search themselves, to confess their sins and to exhort others to do the same. It was only natural that people would remember loved ones who had died, so visions occurred of family and friends in heaven, comforting those who remained. There was the hope that they would eventually be reunited, thus ending the emotional pain of separation.

Very few of the female experiences of the Ulster Revival were recorded, but from the little that we know it is apparent that women adopted religious behaviour for a number of reasons. Some believe that the women were attracted to Christianity as a result of mental anxiety; if this were so, it was more likely to be occasioned by the constant presence of death rather than any other cause. Women did not see their conversions as an escape from the miseries of industrialisation. The idea that the women were simply reacting to economic stress ignores evidence that women acted assertively and used the revival as a way to achieve personal goals and aspirations.

Another category of visions apparently had little to do with Christianity. The visions were extremely sensational and they suggest that it was a time of emotional chaos. Five years earlier the ministers would have condemned such visions outright. Even during the revival Anglican priests represented a strong body of criticism. However, the working classes considered these visions and miracles credible, and those who experienced them were keenly sought after. Clerical condemnation had little effect. People flocked to see those who had been stricken, and they attended meetings in the hope that they too would be affected in a similar way. They believed that to be saved one had to be physically stricken. Women formed the vanguard of the movement, and some of the most unusual of the visions were associated with women.

One of the most common features of this type of vision was a type of clairvoyance where the subject would fall into a trance-like state. Mary Ann was nineteen years old. She lived at Drummaul, County Antrim. She was a Presbyterian and regularly attended Sunday school. She was stricken down on 30 June 1859. She began to pray with great fervour for half an hour. When finished she arose exclaiming that she would be deprived of sight, speech and hearing until noon the following day. She cried out that God would be with her; God would pour out His grace on to her soul. She closed her eyes, her teeth went together with a snap, and she became motionless. Upon hearing of this, hundreds of people crowded around her, convinced that she had been favoured by Christ. When she awoke those that had gathered were interested in what she had seen, but Mary Ann rebuked them for their curiosity and told them nothing.

Other visions portrayed heaven and hell, depicting the spiritual battle that was taking place between Satan and Jesus. Hell was described by one woman as a burning lake. As she was passing by it, the gates of hell flew open, and she saw burning mountains of fire. The path leading to the lake was very dark and slippery.

Margaret Martin and Elizabeth Dumigan, both of Portadown, claimed to have been visited by evil angels dressed in black, who tempted them to forsake Christ and physically abused them. Elizabeth prayed until good angels arrived dressed in white. The good angels vanquished the evil angels and comforted her with the assurance of Jesus's love and care.

Some of the visions were even more fanciful. Rose Ann Wilson of Christopher Street, Belfast, said that she would fall into a trance on 24 August, and it would last for thirty-six hours. While she was stricken down, a crowd gathered, waiting for her to wake. She regained consciousness, but remained deaf and dumb. She motioned for writing materials so that she could relate her experiences. Rose Ann claimed to have seen fireballs in the sky, and a gentleman from the London City Mission who was present verified her report. He said he had seen ten such fireballs, but others who were there claimed to have seen even more fireballs than that.

The most serious cases of physical manifestation occurred in mid-September 1859. This is known as the Marks Controversy. Words such as God and Jesus, letters, and religious symbols such as a cross were imprinted on women's chests or upper arms, usually while in a trance. These manifestations were widely condemned, even in newspapers that were quite open-minded about such events. Women believed that the marks had a divine origin, whilst the clergy claimed they had been painted on. Newspapers were critical for a variety of reasons, the first being that these women were charging admission to see the marks. Clairvoyance was an easier occupation than honest labour. Newspapers also pointed out what they felt to be the blatant Catholic overtones to this phenomenon. It was said that the marks had a resemblance to the stigmata, and that good Protestant readers should leave superstition to Roman Catholics. The *Ballymena Observer* was willing to admit that the women might have been duped – the marks might have been imprinted while they were unconscious – but it was impossible to determine the truth of these visions or the purpose that they served. For those involved, reasons did not appear to be necessary.

These great events were considered to be part of the revival atmosphere. Instead of viewing the revival as the source of the manifestations, it is possible to see it as a means of removing some of the cultural prohibitions and restrictions associated with religious practice at that time. Thus the manifestations reveal a popular attitude to Christianity in a time of upheaval. The visions helped the women to believe in direct interaction of the infinite with their limited lives.

The women of the Marks Controversy exhibited the marks on their bodies as a result of confrontations with evil angels; they felt Satan trying to push them from the narrow path. They saw supernatural lights in a darkened church, and fireballs appeared out of heaven and hovered over them. These experiences were connected with a variety of beliefs, which included Christian concepts as well as folklore and popular superstition, despite the efforts of the clergy to train their congregations in Christian doctrine.

Recent theories have tried to show that increasing industrialisation and modernisation made it possible for people to believe in the supernatural world existing above the natural one. The revival was supposed to affect the transition to this new rationalistic religion. Instead the Ulster Revival only revealed the continued existence of superstition and supernatural beliefs amongst the majority of the population, including city-dwellers. These visions allowed women to exercise themselves in a way that would not normally be acceptable.

Spectacular visitations might have increased the reputation of the women visionaries amongst ordinary people, but they were condemned by the clergy. It was obvious that those affected had a very special religious experience.

Rose Ann Wilson was asked to describe what she had seen and to predict the spread of the revival; she was also asked to lead a group in hymn-singing and prayer. Her experiences could not be challenged. Rose Ann obtained a measure of authority and leadership that she could not have achieved elsewhere.

The revival presented the opportunity for such experiences to be regarded as legitimate – as part of a deeply personal relationship with Christ. It also acted as an encouragement for women's rights. Women could go to God with their very special desires; they no longer had to put up with men in their lives. The clergy had traditionally been the interpreters of God's will in society through their sermons, church discipline and Holy Communion, but the spectacular visions bypassed the system, eliminating the ministers from any sort of power. The clergy were rendered powerless in the face of the visions. To claim that the visions were false was to challenge the character of the women, the nature of the experience, and the revival's claim for a divine origin. To retain some degree of leadership, clergymen were forced to acknowledge these phenomena, but they did so reluctantly.

Women and their role in society were influenced by two contradictory forces: first, the liberating force of conversions that stressed spiritual equality based on a shared experience in Christianity; and secondly, the restrictive force of a society preoccupied with respectability. Conversion could bless anyone, and from then on the dividing line between people was redrawn between the 'saved' and the 'unsaved'. Revival writers noted that one of the characteristics of conversion was the immediate desire to tell others about their experiences. There was a dramatic increase in the amount of lay involvement in the many meetings, from praying aloud to exhortation. Some of the meetings were conducted without the presence of a minister. Women took advantage of a weakening of restrictions on their participation in order to exercise leadership roles.

Unlike England, Ireland had only a limited experience of female preachers. Alice Cambridge preached in Irish Methodist circles from 1780 to 1826, having her greatest success in Ulster. Anne Lutton, another Methodist, preached at over 169 meetings in twenty-seven places during the course of 1813–31. Her audiences were restricted to women, in keeping with the 1803 ruling of the Methodist Conference. Men sometimes tried to enter her meetings by gathering around the church windows or hiding in the galleries, or even dressing in women's clothes. Irish clergy were therefore not used to women's spiritual leadership. When the revival provided women with opportunities to preach in mixed company, ministers were some of their most outspoken opponents.

What was meant by *preaching*? Olive Anderson defines it as the deliberate undertaking of women to evangelise, to perform spiritual instruction in mixed public assemblies held for that purpose, with no attempt to disguise the activities of their congregation.

But little female preaching took place during the Ulster Revival. Miss McKinny of Fintona, County Tyrone, preached in Corporation Hall, Londonderry, in October 1859. The novelty of having a female preacher attracted a large congregation, and the hall was filled to capacity. Miss Buck of Leicester preached in the Victoria Hall in Belfast, in October, to help to raise funds for schools in connection with Melbourne Street Primitive Methodist Church. This points to the fact that female preaching could have taken place on both a local and a national level, but the small amount of evidence makes any generalised conclusion impossible.

The most famous female to preach in Ulster was the American Methodist Mrs Phoebe Palmer. Whilst on tour with her husband in Britain, she visited Belfast, Coleraine and Antrim to observe the progress of the revival. They addressed several meetings. Dr Palmer spoke first. He was followed by his wife, who stepped forward within the rails of the Communion table, addressing the people in a very solemn manner. She urged upon the Church the necessity for immediate action. Her language was spectacular and effective. The address lasted for about half an hour.

Any formalised preaching only took place in connection with the Irish Methodist Church, but this was rare. Two branches of Methodism supported female preaching – the Bible Christians and the Primitive Methodists.

The level of informal female preaching compensated for the lack of any formalised female leadership.

A stricken woman exhorted those gathered around her to repent, praying for them and quoting from the Bible. The congregation could number from five to over 100 souls, but the average seems to have been about thirty. The females would then lead the group in prayers and Scripture readings. Females also acted as councillors and visitors, helping their local minister to attend to his congregation. For example, the Misses Herley of

Glasgow came over to help the minister at Portrush to comfort his female members.

During the revival female leadership took the form of sharing testimonies at meetings. At the Berry Street gathering of the Presbyterian Church, Belfast, the service had to be dismissed to allow ministers and friends to pray with thirteen people who had been stricken down. One of the spectators found that none of the ministers was able to help, so he suggested that a woman, the first convert to recover, be taken to speak to those who still struggled with their faith. The effect was immediate, for those stricken down had found peace.

Methodist class meetings were amply suitable for this sharing of experience. They were instituted so that the faithful could help one another, and this function continued throughout the revival.

In a more formal setting two women were invited to speak at a meeting held in the Methodist chapel at Londonderry – not to quote Scripture, but to relate their testimonies.

Public addresses involving women were rarely set up with the intention of quoting from the Bible. Many clergy were opposed to the idea of laymen adopting this role, so they could not be expected to approve of females doing the same. Women's addresses therefore took place on an informal level. They exhorted at their own bedsides, and shared some of their personal experiences in the class meetings, and at prayer meetings.

The impact of these leadership opportunities on many women is told in the story of Miss R., who after her conversion travelled around the countryside exhorting people to repent, saying, "The Lord has sent me to bring you to Him; He is waiting for you. Arise and follow me."

People did follow her, and she attracted great crowds.

One day, whilst out walking accompanied by her followers, she met her minister, the Reverend William Magill, who advised her to be silent lest people should think she was mad. He recorded her reply: she drew herself up in a most commanding manner, measuring him from head to foot, and she declared that she was astonished at him. She said that he had instructed her in his Sunday school and Bible class to follow the Lord. She said she could now teach the children, and she would bring them to Jesus. Should she not follow the will of her Father in heaven? She said she was in touch with the Spirit of the Lord. Magill was forced into silence at this. He fell in behind her and became one of her followers.

The nature of this woman's experience urged her to speak out and exhort those around her. Like many female preachers in England, she claimed that the authority of the Holy Spirit justified her actions, so shielding her from criticism. The fact that a man followed her lent further credence to her preaching. The most noted aspect of her preaching was that it was only temporary. According to Magill, after a few days she settled down as a devout follower of Christ, her work completed. She roused the country, and then retired into private life. In the quiet of her family home she and her sisters read the Gospels, conversed on religious topics and praised God. Only during peaks of excitement were her talents called upon.

Once the goal of a revived population had been reached, women like Miss R. were expected to return to their positions as guardians of the home. In the long term, the revival did not alter the moral and spiritual basis of society; it was not a liberating force for women.

There is little evidence to show how women reacted to female leadership roles.

Grace Hunter, from Downpatrick, heard Mrs Phoebe Palmer preach at Belfast. She could not describe her feelings for she was overwhelmed, but she returned the following night and described it as 'a time of power'. She credited Mrs Palmer with being a great influence in her life.

It is impossible to generalise about women from a single

account; but for Grace Hunter, seeing women in a role of spiritual leadership was a significant event.

The wave of religious enthusiasm that accompanied the Ulster Revival temporarily broke down traditional barriers, and Ulsterwomen experienced increased opportunities to exercise their religious feelings in their own way. Women who had visions were considered spiritual 'experts' and especially blessed by God. These women were fitted to speak in front of mixed audiences with little criticism – indeed with outright acceptance by the majority of the laity. Where quoting Scripture was still prohibited, they at least were able to share their conversion experience and encourage others to lead a religious life.

However, a lot of the excitement faded, and with it the mandate for women's leadership roles. Only when the world was turned upside down were their efforts appreciated. The stereotype of women as being spiritual and submissive had been only temporarily abandoned.

Chapter 6

The Temperance Movement

'Modest grace' was referred to, and sentiments like this might sound sad to us today, but to the readers of the *Irish Temperance League Journal* and *Everybody's Monthly* they were part of a shared religious experience. Ulster temperance literature may seem melodramatic or even hysterical, but the subject of alcohol and women was charged in late-Victorian evangelical times.

The model of female piety is fundamentally a paradoxical one. Women were portrayed as possessing real moral power in their roles as guardians of the home. Through the strength of their faith women could determine the future of the nation – whether it would be on the side of righteousness or fall into ungodliness. However, women were portrayed as morally and physically weak. Their faith and virtue, their chief weapons against demon drink, were fragile indeed. Marilyn Westerhamp has recently described this in the following manner: Gender analysis understands gender as a primary category for social and historical interpretations under investigation. It explores social systems operating within the community in terms of gender as a signifier of power.

Women were silent creatures, and the pages of temperance literature were overflowing with images of virtuous, self-sacrificing women, who through sheer dint of their holy example could save those who had turned to drink. Christian women would only have a significant influence for good if they themselves were suitable for the task.

At the annual meeting of the Belfast Ladies' Temperance Union in May 1884, the Reverend J. Waddell spoke about female piety: women were amply suited to temperance work for they were blessed with a true moral perception. They saw the light at once and they did not allow their judgement to be altered in regard to consequences. Women pronounced in favour of what was just. Their heightened moral sensitivity and natural piety could play a useful role in the transatlantic evangelical temperance movement, which included Ireland. Male Ulster temperance advocates frequently praised their female workers for their innate spirituality and pious feelings.

While women's influence was mentioned in temperance literature, for some time they did not have temperance organisations of their own. The most well-known temperance organisation to which women belonged was the Belfast Ladies' Temperance Union, which began in 1862 and reorganised as the Belfast Women's Temperance Association in 1874. Both of these organisations had their headquarters at Belfast. Although there were affiliated branches throughout Ireland, they were mainly concentrated in Ulster.

An article in the February edition of the *Irish Temperance League Journal*, entitled 'Women's Work', described the origins of the Belfast Women's Temperance Association. It was founded on 10 May 1874, and since then had been engaged in various branches of temperance work, and had spread itself out in many different directions. Since 1874 forty-nine branches of the association had been established throughout Ireland; indeed, almost from one end of Ireland to the other, branch associations had been formed and kept a regular correspondence with the parent association at Belfast. The article mentioned that the Belfast committee members must have abstaining homes and be personal abstainers themselves. The personal influence of women over their children, servants, husbands and other members of their households was considered their most significant contribution to the temperance cause.

The female readers of temperance literature would not have been surprised when told they had an enormous influence over men, other women and children in their care. There were notions of 'power behind the throne', and 'behind every great man is a great woman' – an attitude that was still prevalent in this period. The notion of children as tabulae rasae, upon which personal influence could be exerted without impediment, was somewhat more recent, but it was none the less powerful.

The role of the mother was paramount.

In a story in the *Youth Temperance Banner* entitled 'Home and Mother', a young boy called Harry made his way home from a friend's house despite a threatening storm, but the thought of home urged him on. The mother watched at her window. At length the home was reached, and all the boy's hopes were realised. The two words *home* and *Mother* were Harry's watchwords all through the perilous times from boyhood to manhood. They led him safely through dangers far greater than those which beset him on that windy night. When other boys asked him to join in their night adventures, the thought of his mother by her oil lamp caused him to give a decided "No". He told them they should think about their own mothers and their teachings well and often. Harry's mother had left a light in the window for him. She told him not to turn away from the holy light lest he might fall upon the dark mountain. The mother's pious teachings and moral attitude made her a beacon of light for her children.

The pages of temperance periodicals are full of examples of

Christian motherhood. Mothers were depicted as a conduit of grace, through which sin could be avoided and the sinner could be saved.

A piece of advice was published in *The Puritan*, an American magazine, forty years previously. It was reprinted in the March issue of the *Irish Temperance League Journal*. There was plenty of information about the role of women in it. The anonymous author noted that a woman should promote temperance by example, but it was on children that a woman's influence should be most noticed. They were like pieces of clay, to be moulded by the mother. In short, a mother should remember in bringing up her children to practise virtue. She had a double duty to look after her children's bodies and their minds. If she was successful, she would be a blessed example to future generations. This shows the mother as a powerful force in the construction of a nation's piety. A woman's influence over her children was held to be second to none – an influence that could affect future generations.

A woman's moral influence over her husband was a repeated theme in the Irish temperance movement. The temperance advocates, male and female, clerical and lay, all felt that women's influence was important, and they were always careful to couch it in language that was acceptable to evangelicalism. According to St Paul, Christ was head of the Church and the Church was His bride. In the same way, wives should submit to the leadership of their husbands. Despite this, the innate piety of women gives wives the moral authority to redeem and restore errant husbands. Women were not to usurp male authority, but rather by their own moral authority they were to restore their husbands to righteousness.

The Reverend E. E. Wilmott wrote a temperance poem outlining how this process should work. The poem started with a description of Johnny McCree's ideal marriage, which was going to ruin, for Johnny liked something stronger than tea. According to the third verse, he had a good little wife and she was sober and tidy; she washed his clothes and cared for him, but it was all labour marred, for he liked the drink. By the seventh first he was drinking away his wages and coming home drunk, causing his wife a good deal of worry. When she got him into bed, she wept, but the big tears of grief gave her little relief, for he still liked to drink. In her sorrow Nancy turned to God and prayed that her husband would be saved, but like a kind and prudent wife she avoided all trouble, not criticising her husband. These tactics eventually proved successful and Johnny at last was saved. He abstained from alcohol, and he was now content with a cup of tea. It should be noted how explicitly it was stated that Mrs McCree did not harass her husband or criticise his behaviour. She used moral persuasion.

Women were informed by temperance writers that their gentle forbearance was essential if they were to succeed in evangelical circles. The usurpation of the husband's role was not allowed, even though the righteousness of their anti-drink campaign afforded women a high moral authority. Gentle persuasion should be used, they said, because it fitted traditional gender norms and because it worked.

Male temperance writers acknowledged the role that women played in their lives. The latest theories explaining their propensity to turn the tables of gender authority upside down in this way shall be mentioned, but at the moment let us examine their notion of female strengths. In an article in the first edition of the league's journal, entitled 'Words for Wives', the editor, William Church, had the following advice to give to his female readers. He said that the influence of a wife should play a key role, and that there was not a woman living that was not day by day influencing her husband's career. The men were foolishly proud, and did not like the way their wives were influencing them, but they knew that, outside of their business, all their doings were more or less controlled by their wives. They said it was a disgrace for a man to be kept at home, away from bad company, away from bad pleasure and foolish expense. Some poor souls agreed, but a guardian angel stood between them and ruin.

Several decades of the *Irish Temperance League Journal* did not uncover a single voice rising up to contradict these beliefs. It seems to have been universally accepted in evangelical circles that women wielded a powerful influence over their husbands, but the power was not political or physical; rather it was moral and spiritual. Whether this constitutes what modern females call real power is not an issue here. What is important is that the authors of the evangelical women's movement depicted women as having considerable moral authority and power.

Frequently in temperance fiction (the vast majority written by women) the heroine actually martyred herself in order to hold a hand out to an unrepentant man. Heroines in these tales were usually wives, mothers, sisters or daughters of alcoholic men. The presence of drink in the home caused the moral decline of the head of the family, usually resulting in the women's 'fading' or 'sinking', but their wife's holy, patient and virtuous example, often at the point of death, had the effect of shaming the male alcoholic into repentance.

In a story called 'A Narrow Escape', written by Mrs Bewsher, a popular writer of temperance fiction, the heroine, Martha Newton, made just such a sacrifice. When she discovered that her husband had started to drink, she tried to undo the mischief that bad company had wrought. She made the home as cheerful as possible, for she realised how filthy the menfolk could be. Martha must have read temperance literature, for she knew a bright household would tame the men; the household should be a welcoming place. Other temperance poems often focused on the theme of women's duties, one of which was to brighten homes with pleasant smiles, but this was not sufficient for the Newton household. Mr Newton's drinking worsened, and Martha's health deteriorated because of his attitude to her. There was no suggestion of physical abuse, but violence was often the cause of suffering and sometimes death for the wives of alcoholics in Victorian times. Martha became seriously ill – death stalked the house – but she was not to be pitied. Her great afflictions had led her to Christ – to prayer, the weapon of the Christian on the battlefield of life. She warned her husband, once again, not to give way to drink. Despite the gravity of her illness, her dominant thought was that he should realise the awful sin of excessive drinking and change his ways. Fortunately for her husband, these were not Martha's final words; rather she told him of the Lord's mercy and saving grace. Anguish filled his soul; he saw his vileness and accused himself of being his wife's killer. At length Mrs Newton begged for God's mercy. Even though Martha died, her suffering was, according to the dictates of Christianity, worthwhile as it brought her to a very personal relationship with God.

Mrs Bewsher instructed readers that it was her husband that should be pitied; if he had died unrepentant, he would have faced damnation. As a result of Martha's Christian example, Mr Newton had a narrow escape. The reader was not meant to experience pity for Martha's fate, for she had triumphed and fulfilled her role as a Christian woman to the greatest degree.

Not only adult women, but also female children, were said to have a powerful influence over those caught in the grip of demon drink. The following story, entitled 'What Love Can Do', illustrates this in a typically Victorian way. The author was a temperance worker who said that the story had a beautiful moral. One can wonder at the fidelity of the dear child, even more than at the cruelty of the father. The heroine of the tale is little Millie, whose father was a drunkard. She had tried to persuade him to come home with her, but she was a martyr to her faith and returned to her cabin, dark and silent. Events took place over weeks and months, but the father persisted in his drunkenness. One day when he awoke from slumber after a binge, he found her preparing breakfast for him and singing a childlike song.

He turned to her and asked her in a tender tone what made her stay with him.

She replied that it was because he was her father and she loved him.

He replied in astonishment, "You love me? What makes you love me?"

He was a poor drunkard, and everyone despised him. Why did she not do so?

The girl replied with swimming eyes that her mother had taught her to love him, and every night she came from heaven and stood by her little bed, and said, "Millie, don't leave your father. He will go away from that drink fiend some day." She told Millie that when he gave up drink she would be happy.

The quiet persistent love of this child brought happiness for this man. Thus the persistent love of this female child, and the love of a great Christian mother from beyond the grave, had an awesome saving power.

These are but a few examples of the persuasive nature of temperance literature. Women were seen to be suited for this saving role because of their good nature and enormous capacity for love. It was stated, 'Oh, woman, whoever you may be, remember that your influence is great.' One kind word from a woman might save a drunkard. What would the world be like without an affectionate female? The word had risen for the erring. It protected the weak, and it's working will never cease until the last woman's heart has ceased to beat over the last object of her pity.

This passionate declaration of women's capacity for compassion underlined the moral authority of women. So strong was this perception of female moral power that when clerics and other activists felt that women were not pulling their weight they started to criticise. In the following example, the belief in women's powerful moral influence was again stated, but it was also implied that by not doing all they could they were standing in the way of temperance. The female author of this piece entitled 'Women's Rights', printed in the *Irish Templar*, encouraged her readers by stating that the women of Ireland had a duty to exercise their godliness at home. Some women might say, in apathy, that boys will be boys, but the boys would soon be men, and the question was, what sort of men would they be? Women had a duty to influence their sons.

Pleas for women to do their duty and to wield their moral influence for the temperance cause were not always moderate. Editorials heaped scorn upon women who did not exert a moral influence over their children. The temperance movement was attempting to further reinforce their notion of the power of female piety, while attempting to regulate and channel that power.

The Reverend John Pyper, in an article praising the good work of the Belfast Ladies' Temperance Union, made the following remarks: Observation teaches us that not only were thousands standing aloof from men, who had special claims upon their sympathy, but no other human agency had the ability to contribute so greatly to the sum of domestic happiness; the movement had few more serious hindrances in its way than the wives and daughters of Ireland. There were luckily many honourable exceptions; amongst these the glorious cause had no more devoted workers than the Belfast Ladies' Temperance Union.

Those that contributed to female moral authority did not hesitate to castigate women who were not up to their level of moral piety.

According to temperance writers, women had many strengths, but they had many weaknesses also. The physical weakness of women was linked with their moral failings. Biology was destiny. From the same temperance author, who exhorted her sisters to further activism, the following view was given: a drunken woman was even worse than a drunken man. The delicacy of her system was in itself enough to enable her to feel the seriousness of her sins. Men would do much to get drunk, but they had never known a man to do what a woman had done. She had done things that could not be surpassed, and which no man could equal. The constitution of the female body, its delicacy and sensitiveness accounts for this situation. Words could not describe the condition of a female drunk. It shocked everyone and was the exact opposite of what a women should be.

Temperance was essential. It struck at the very essence of womanhood. However, women because of their weakness were highly susceptible, so they required the teaching of orthodox Christianity. Christian medical warnings and godly legislation were paramount.

A paper delivered by the Reverend William Caine, a former chaplain at the Manchester Prison, to a Belfast meeting of the Economic Science and Statistics section of the British Temperance Association, condemned the use of alcohol. He stated that female drunkenness was increasing by an alarming extent – 60 per cent in four years – and their drinking often led to other crimes. Plutarch said that in the early ages of Rome women were strictly prohibited from tasting wine; other early writers said women were punished with death for drunkenness, just as if they had committed adultery.

When, he asked, would English legislators be as wise as Romulus and Numa to discourage women from drinking alcohol? It appeared that men following Jesus permitted women, who ought to be models of everyday life, to sink into alcoholism. Old Romulus and Numa, on the other hand, stopped women from even tasting this poison – alcohol – which could lead to fatal results.

The writer who reported this speech in the pages of the *Irish Temperance League Journal* did not mention the significant fact that the all-male audience had responded with a heavy heart – "Hear! hear!" – at this stage of the meeting.

The Reverend Caine went on to describe the sex ratios of the inmates of Manchester Prison. Not surprisingly, they presented shocking evidence of female depravity. However, it was depravity of a very special nature. The Protestant inmates charged to Caine's care were predominantly male. He lamented the predicament of the Catholic chaplain, Father Nugent, who had the task of administering to the spiritual needs of a total of 12,420 inmates, the majority of whom were women. The Reverend Caine did not point out that the difference between the numbers of Catholic and Protestant women was only a matter of 5.4 per cent. More females than males were incarcerated for drunkenness. In view of this, it was impossible to avoid the conclusion that Catholics were more depraved than Protestants. In only one instance was there a placard stating that women drunkards were more depraved than men.

In the September 1877 edition of the *Irish Temperance League Journal* an article, 'A Woman's Protest and Impeachment', condemned the sexual double standards in respect to drink. It was stated that a different standard of morality was wanted in the country, and that was Christ's standard. There was no sex in guilt, in crime. It was not good that a man should be drunk, as for a woman. "Oh, young men," it was said, "you must now sow your wild oats, but let it be remembered that whatever a man sows he will reap." The law of nature and of God could not be challenged. A public sentiment should be created that would require conformity on the part of men as well as women.

This was not, however, the consensus on the issue; for most temperance writers, female intemperance was more morally condemned than male intemperance. The tragedy of female drunkenness, the ease with which women could fall victim to drink, and the measures necessary to remedy this were all topics of temperance fiction. These stories were mainly penned by female writers. Scientific and medical opinion was on the side of temperance advocates. Women writers pointed out the horrors of female intemperance in a highly repetitive fashion in temperance literature, and they were supported by male experts in the temperance movement.

A serialised story by Mrs M. A. Paull, 'Our Bill at the Grocers', was described as 'Founded on fact – the plight of a young husband and father, Anthony, whose wife had become an alcoholic.' The wife had deserted her husband and young children, and Anthony and informed his elder brother James of his troubles. He was deserted and his children were worse than motherless. The state of his house had deteriorated since James last saw it. There was never a better mistress of a poor man's home than existed before Anthony's wife took to drink, and he said she never should have gone to a pub in the beginning. Anthony told his brother that he gave his wife money to buy boots for their handicapped child, and, in an act betraying her motherhood, she had bought drink with it instead. Anthony told James that it was nearly midnight when she returned to the house, a drunken woman instead of the honoured, sober and industrious wife he had loved and cherished. If ever strong drink made an incarnate fiend out of a gentlewoman it was then, he said. He could hardly trace in that fiery-eyed, bold-faced woman the idol of his early manhood, the beloved, trusted, tender wife of earlier days.

There was no salvation for Anthony's wife, for she had subverted the moral code as a wife and mother. For a woman who stepped outside the boundaries of the model of female piety there was little hope.

The author of 'Womanly Influence' explained that she had known cases of men who, without seeking God's grace, had by their own will become sober men again. On the other hand, a woman's nature was more highly strung, and she had so much more need for the love of God.

This theme was brought home many times in temperance literature. Men could have narrow escapes and return to the straight and narrow, but it was much harder for women to return to the straight path. The reports of temperance missions, who visited jails and distributed temperance literature, portrayed women drinkers as almost impossible to save.

In the tragic temperance poem 'A Woman's Story', by Rosina Sadler, the moral, that women were reduced by the effects of drink, came across in a very powerful way. The wife and mother in the story falls ill with fever, and during her recovery she is prescribed brandy, though many condemned the use of alcohol in medicine as immoral. She takes to drinking heavily and her infant son dies of neglect; then her husband falls prey to the peculiar malady that afflicted those living in households where drink was available. From the time of the death of the baby, her husband began to fade, and, like her other son, he was soon on his deathbed. His wife knew that his heart, so good and true, was affected with a sense of shame.

The entire spectrum of female behaviour was thus revealed, from the ideal of the woman who had sacrificed all for those she had loved to its perverted mirror image, the woman who sacrificed the one she had loved because of her addiction to alcohol. Using her moral persuasion and gentle influence a woman should be part of the Christian crusade against sin; but once she is lost to sin herself, she is the ultimate sinner, casting down not only herself, but also her husband, her children, her community and her nation. Women's influence was a two-edged sword. It could earn her the highest praise, but when she failed she became a scandal.

In the background of the evangelical situation was a sometimes dark and shadowy distorted image of Irish Catholic women. In papers with a wide circulation, like the *Irish Temperance League Journal*, which praised Catholic temperance efforts, reports of drunken Catholic women were only found in articles by experts, like the Reverend Caine. The sectarian ugliness was covered up by a veil of science. As far as fiction was concerned, the Protestant writers of the journal were not circumspect. In a play called *Comparisons*, John Bull (a reformer) and Paddy Erin met several times. Paddy's wife, Biddy, was everything evangelical women were not. The Erins' home was filthy, and John Bull said that a pailful of whitewash for your walls was far better than a drink of whiskey for your bodies. Paddy replied that Biddy was of the opinion that whiskey was life itself. Instead of advocating moderation, Biddy Erin encouraged her family to drink. Unlike Johnny McCree's wife, who did not scold her husband, Biddy delighted in upbraiding the helpless Paddy. She continued to scold him about his bad manners, ignored his opinions, and dominated almost every scene she was in. Unlike the gentle heroines of the temperance tales, Biddy Erin never held her tongue. She left the stage, as she entered, with a cloud of oaths, chasing after a goat who Biddy said was like her master, Paddy, for there was no teaching her manners. Although Biddy Erin was a comic figure, in her personality there was a domineering facet of womanhood that Protestants did not like and even feared. She bragged about her darling son, and she said one day he might reach Parliament – he would earn a name for himself. Perhaps Biddy Erin was a kind of negative reference point, encouraging conservative evangelicals who feared the Catholic majority to portray even more rigorously their women as completely different from those whom they feared.

In many articles enlisting the support of women for the temperance cause, it was stated that women were the greatest victims of intemperance. Women were said to suffer the most because of drink. In an appeal for women's influence and aid, one author said that wife-beating and murder were associated with drink. Vast was the number of wives and mothers, daughters and sisters who suffered silently, no ear hearing what was being said, no eye seeing what they had to endure. What misery females had to endure because of intemperance! – broken hearts, wasted bodies, downtrodden love, disappointed hopes. If only women could see what drink had done to other women in our land, they would raise the voice of warning and employ the most persuasive arguments to turn men from it, as from the cup of misery and death.

This appeal was addressed to women's natural compassion. The following statement appealed to the more practical concern of self-interest. It was said that nowhere was the evil of drink more painfully felt than within domestic circles – a woman's kingdom, her state, her world. Where females exercised their most refined influences the bane of intemperance was most keenly felt. If there was no other reason why ladies should throw their influence into the total-abstinence cause, they could not help thinking that this was an all-sufficient one. Self-defence, and the defence of all that was dear, should enlist every woman in the ranks of personal abstinence.

It would be a grave error to interpret these statements simply as a manifestation of evangelical self-interest. There is little doubt that drink caused women and children much suffering. While paternalism, class prejudice and self-interest may have informed the evangelical temperance movement in Ulster, one should not be too quick to dismiss movements of compassion and Christian love. The testimonials of female workers show the great concern these females felt for those they called the victims of drink.

Ministers, laymen and laywomen all contributed extensively to this model of evangelical female piety. A major concern that arose was about this alliance of interests. The clergy presented women as more pious than men, and this may seem strange at first; but when we realise women's contributions to the evangelical foundations under adverse conditions this phenomenon seems less surprising. Women, who were the chief victims of drink, needed temperance, and the temperance cause needed women. This construction of female piety was not static; it changed over a period of time.

The work of female anti-alcohol campaigners in the United

States was well covered in Irish temperance literature. Mrs Stewart arrived in Belfast for a series of meetings in 1874. She was the leader of the Women's Whisky War in Ohio. She and her associates were greeted with a great fanfare. Anna Maria Hall, an English temperance advocate, wrote in the *Alliance News* that the work of these heroic women in Ohio and other states was essential for women's work. They were doing it not by usurping the role of men but with weapons that were essentially female – by persuasion and prayer. God gave them fruit of the seed they were planting.

Those that awaited the arrival in the United Kingdom of these American temperance ladies frequently drew attention to what American women were doing: denouncing male clergy for their inaction and holding hymn-singing and prayer meetings inside the saloons and bars. This was somewhat unwomanly, according to the construction just seen, with its emphasis on gentle persuasion. They were clearly outside the accepted evangelical gender conformity, but the American activists and their Irish supporters went to some lengths to convince others, and perhaps to convince themselves, that this was not the case. Every article emphasised that they were not usurping the male role, and that they were not dreadful Amazons. As Westerhamp pointed out in her study of female puritanism, dissonance was created when those who by gender definition should have no authority became spiritually empowered. In this case the American women who headed God's call gained spiritual authority, but this was very disturbing for Ulster evangelists. Amazonian women, they felt, were out of place in the notion of female piety that had evolved in Ulster.

A number of letters were printed in the *Irish Temperance League Journal* anticipating the women's arrival. One particular letter from the United States is a good indicator of the radical nature of the female crusade. It said that the reformers would use persuasion, but not prayers, and the writer said that this made the women brazen-faced, that it took away their dignity, and that it gave the young a dominating manner and bold appearance.

Lovers of order trembled, but progress marched onward.

When the American women reached London, Francis Craig wrote a report for temperance people in Ireland. Craig described how 'Mother' Stewart, this radical woman, conformed to the evangelical model of piety: her voice was sweet, but not loud, it was clear and sometimes penetrating. One's heart goes out to Mother Stewart, standing and pleading for her righteous cause. Her eyes were flashing, and her ardent feelings brightened her face. Now and then her voice would falter just a little to prove how womanly she was.

At the Annual Soirée of the Irish Temperance League, held at Belfast in April 1876, Mrs Stewart was the key speaker, and she had many inspiring words to say. The time had come when the Master had called his handmaidens to take a stand against evil. The gentlemen friends of the temperance cause had laboured for years against great opposition, but the missing link was the women. Now, if only Christ would inspire them, the women of Ireland might rise up in a leadership role. There was applause; although men had a prejudice against women taking part in public meetings, they still acknowledged the role of women. Women sometimes felt that they were helpless. They had seen their friends sacrificed, and they had seen hearts and homes broken, yet they felt powerless. Traditionally women were not meant to be out of their place doing anything, but the ideal of womanhood had been exalted to a false standard. The real woman was a true follower of Christ, ready to help and relieve suffering everywhere. This message was an assault on the construction that temperance journals were advocating. Mrs Stewart said that women should not be relegated to a secondary role in the domestic sphere, for it was not natural or divinely ordained. She attacked what she called a false standard. Mrs

Stewart understood that her own role was an orthodox one, but her orthodoxy lay in her being spiritually empowered by her own strength and through God's love. She said that it was time all obstacles were removed, and women should be allowed to come forward and help if they could. It was not for her to advise, for that was God's role. When God saw them ready, He would inspire the hearts of his handmaidens. She called upon them, in the name of the souls that were threatened, to rise up in the might that God had given them and fight evil. She called upon her sisters to go forth and take a stand.

How did the Ulster Christians respond to these challenges and to this overturning of their expected ideas about female piety – this call for women to leave their gradualism and gentle methods of reform?

Mrs Margaret Byers had the following comments to make when delivering the 1878 annual report to the Belfast Women's Temperance Association. She said that the committee had nothing new to report about the working of the association. Its plans had been carried on in a quiet way, but its action had been nonetheless powerful for good despite being characterised by nothing sensational. This was a clear repudiation of Mrs Stewart's call for women to abandon gentle reform under godly influence. The American method of shocking women into awareness of the evils of intemperance was rejected by Ulster's single most influential evangelical female. She stated that work with female prisoners was popular with women of the Belfast Women's Temperance Association because they were deeply touched by the degraded condition of poor women, the victims of drink. They had been cast out by society, and disowned by their own relations, but they would be given a chance of recovery.

Clearly, proper outlets for women's compassion did not include criticising the failures of the Church hierarchy or staging demonstrations masquerading as hymn-singing on the doorsteps of public houses. The way of Ulsterwomen was to use their moral influence in their homes and amongst other women.

Some indication of Mrs Byers' reasoning may be found in the latter part of the report. She credits the daughters of the famous anti-slavery advocates with great influence over their fathers' political and social activities. In the same way, many statesmen and many authors, many professional men and many businessmen had great zeal in temperance work, stimulated by the gentle approval and sympathy of women. Though they might shrink from public work, these women influenced at their own firesides.

The effective alliance between evangelical clergy and women gave some satisfaction to both its constituent groups. For women the main benefits of this alliance might at first be difficult to discern. The way in which the temperance movement was implemented in Ulster assured it of an enlargement of activity, from their own homes to the homes of other women, to public places where they could aid other females.

However, this ideology of evangelical femininity was restricted. Male elites might take comfort in the thought that their women were imbibing a set of prescriptions that warned of the danger of stepping outside convention. This seemed to give men power over women, who were taught that submission to the dictates of the male hierarchy, both clerical and lay, was in their best interests and, moreover, that their subjection was sanctioned by Christ.

Chapter 7

Women in Convents

Convents flourished in Ulster from the middle of the nineteenth century. Nuns were a familiar sight in the town and villages of Ulster. During the period 1840–1940 convents sprang up across the seven Catholic dioceses of the north of Ireland.

The growth of convents in Ulster between 1840 and 1940 was part of a general trend in the Catholic Church in Ireland at this time. Archbishop (later Cardinal) Paul Cullen was the driving force at the head of this movement for the regeneration of Catholicism until his death in 1878. Cullen was an ultramontane, and he contributed to the growing influence of the Pope in Irish Catholicism. The collapse of the European monarchies, along with rapidly improving systems of communications, and innovations in the postal service, railways and shipping, increased his ability to supervise. The Cardinal was determined to improve the internal discipline of the Irish Church and to bring it into line with European Catholicism.

Following the potato famine of the mid-nineteenth century the population of Ireland dropped considerably. As a result, a programme of improvement was made possible within the Irish Church. New churches were built, colourful vestments were worn, and more frequent sacraments and religious ceremonies were established. In 1840 the ratio of priests to parishioners in Ireland stood at 1: 3,500; by 1870 the ratio had dropped to 1:1,250. These improving conditions were reflected in the growing numbers of female religious. In 1800 there were as few as 120 nuns in all of Ireland. By 1851 this figure had risen to 1,500, and it had multiplied to 8,000 women by the close of the nineteenth century. For women from respectable backgrounds, joining a convent was one of the few occupations open to them. By the 1911 census, nuns outnumbered teachers, midwives and nurses.

The growth of the Catholic middle class during 1840–1940, with the improving economic conditions, meant that Catholics were able to improve their status in Ulster society. As a result of Cullen and the ultramontanes, the influence was a conservative one, which included a specific perception of women and their role in the community. Eibhlin Breathnach stated that the notion of women's role in the mid-nineteenth century was derived from two influences. One was rooted in devotion to the Virgin Mary. The behavioural patterns for Irishwomen were obvious – the devoted wife and mother; the chaste virgin, remaining unmarried as a member of a religious house; or the sinner. To reinforce these feminine stereotypes there was a continuous flow of pastoral warnings from the churches, alerting the people to the dangers of giving in to temptation. Sex was equated with sin. In an age when there was a deluge of magazines, books and newspapers, traditional standards were eroded, and public statements about the Roman Catholic Church became increasingly critical.

Post-famine Ireland witnessed an unprecedented rise in the number of women entering convents, due not only to the pressures imposed on women but also to economic conditions in Ulster and their impact on female employment. In pre-famine times women made up half the total agricultural labour force, and to a large extent they were economically independent. J. J. Lee has argued that the famine destroyed much of the cottage industries that the women relied upon, as well as increasing the domestic work they were required to undertake. This led to a decline in their economic status and, as a result, marriage levels dropped. Without the prospect of independence or marital security, large numbers of women emigrated – about 50 per cent of the total emigrating. Many others joined convents. All these women were the victims of an increasingly male-dominated society. Women were expected to be dutiful, passive and obedient, and unmarried women were expected to be sexless.

Restrictive models of female behaviour promoted by a morally conservative Church hierarchy, combined with worsening economic conditions, pushed more and more women into conventional activity. This was a trend experienced throughout Catholic Europe. In 1850 there were seventy-two convents in the Netherlands; by 1900 there were 423. France had 31,000 female religious in 1831; by 1878 the number had increased to 127,000. In Ulster the emerging Catholic middle classes welcomed vocations among their female relatives as a symbol of prestige. Women often entered convents as a way of achieving economic security.

The nuns embarked upon a variety of social, educational and medicinal occupations, and they were responsible for a wide range of institutions – for example, poor schools, night schools, teacher-training colleges, orphanages, homes for the old and infirm, workhouses, reformatories and hospitals – but few ministers acknowledged the professional and practical nature of their work. The men denied women access to powerful positions in the Church. Men controlled those aspects of female convent organisations which might threaten their hegemony. Thus tight control went so far as to include the wording of a female order's constitution. For instance, the 'Propaganda Fides' of the Sisters of Mercy congregation in 1840 said that constitutions cannot be said to be complete when they lack positive prescriptions for observation for the guidelines of order which were necessary for religious communities, especially regarding women. Doubt should be removed along with disquietude and perplexity of the soul.

These were the words of the central body in Rome governing constitutions of Catholic religious communities all over the world. It expressed the male hierarchy belief that women could not exercise power. It also expressed the hierarchy's fear of female religious power in the Church – a fear that would grow as confidence spread throughout Europe and Ireland.

Armagh, Clogher, Derry, Down and Connor, Dromore, Kilmore and Raphoe, the seven Catholic dioceses in Ulster, shared in the massive expansion in the number of new convents from the middle of the nineteenth century to the middle of the twentieth century. This growth had already begun by the time Paul Cullen became a cardinal in 1866. The convents were to play an integral part in raising the profile of Catholicism all over Ireland in the post-famine era. Convents encouraged a wide system of education for the Catholic population of Ulster, as well as providing female agents in orphanages, workhouses, hospitals, old people's homes and reformatories.

In the pre-famine period the hierarchies of the northern dioceses expressed a desire to see convents established in their districts. As early as 1840 the *Irish Catholic Directory and Almanac* contained petitions from bishops of four of the northern dioceses – Clogher, Kilmore, Raphoe, and Down and Connor – asking female congregations to establish branch houses in the north of Ireland. The Most Reverend Cornelius Denvir, Bishop of Down and Connor, stated that he would rejoice to see the introduction of those religious orders which had added so much to the sacred cause of education. At the time there were only two such establishments, both of which were located at Drogheda – the Siena Dominican Convent, St Laurence's Gate, and the Presentation convent, Fair Street. The religious ladies devoted their time and labour to the glory of God and to the good of their neighbours. Both convents ran a school for those in the area, marking a long association between northern convents and education.

Recent history has failed to consider the situation of convents in Ulster in their own right. The convent system, however, flourished in the province and had similar characteristics in the rest of Ireland. Female orders required the permission of the bishop to establish a religious community. In nearly all cases the mother convent would not set up a new convent until a request was made by the local bishop. In 1853 the Most Reverend Cornelius Denvir, Bishop of Down and Connor, sent a deputation of clergy and local businessmen to Dublin's Mercy convent in Baggot Street to make a formal request to establish a convent and a school for the poor at Belfast. The mother superior of the convent, Mother Mary Vincent Whitty, agreed, and on 1 January 1854 three of the sisters moved from Dublin to Belfast – the first nuns in Belfast. They were joined the following day by three more Dublin Sisters of Mercy. They immediately set up a school and started to visit prisoners and the sick, together with running a night school for local working women. A permanent convent was established in the premises known as St Paul's, located on Crumlin Road, Belfast. Their numbers rose quite rapidly. Between 1895 and 1920 there were sixty-four entrants to this one convent. The main growth period was between 1895 and 1905, when fifty new recruits commenced their novitiate.

A similar invitation came from a local bishop. Upon this occasion, Dr Dorrian, the Bishop of Down and Connor, hoped to ease the situation in regard to female education in the rapidly expanding Catholic areas of Belfast. In March 1870 seven Dominican sisters arrived from Cabra to set up a convent on the Falls Road. Four months later they were teaching and managing in St Mary's Convent boarding school. In the following year they also set up their own National School for the poor, St Catherine's.

By 1928 they were teaching at their own teacher-training school. There were also thirty-eight sisters working and living in the congregation, representing more than a fourfold increase.

They were dependent on the male-dominated Catholic hierarchy to grant them permission to expand. Ulster's middle-class Catholics, a group that expanded rapidly in the mid-to-late nineteenth century, were willing contributors, not just of recruits for the religious life but also of money and property. For example, James Duffy, a wealthy Belfast businessman, upon his death in 1854, left £1,000 for the purpose of establishing and maintaining a house to be used by a group of Catholic females for the care of young children. This request facilitated the establishment of the Sisters of Mercy at Belfast.

However, donations from the wealthy were not always very large. To a certain extent schools and convents were said to be self-funded. The main sources of income for the convents were large dowries and money paid to the nuns by the state for the purpose of teaching. Schools were partially financed by the government as part of the national education system.

Dowries were set aside for the personal maintenance of each nun. Dowries from new entrants to the Belfast Mercy convent peaked in 1905. In that year the average contribution from each of the three entrants was about £336, making a total of over £1,000. From 1895 to 1900 there were fifteen new entrants and twelve more in the period 1901–5. Dowries still averaged £320 each. The women would have been from poor families and would have been educated to a lower level than other sisters. The Sisters of Mercy, as well as the Dominicans and other congregations of female religious, divided the new sisters into either lay or choir sisters. The lay sisters would have come from the poorer classes in Ulster and would have had duties pertaining to the upkeep of houses and schools – cleaning, cooking and washing. The choir sisters were generally well educated and would have contributed a large dowry when entering the order. Their duties were of a domestic nature – teaching, nursing, administering and supervising. It was not until 1954 that the Dominican order stopped this policy of lay/choir division; the other orders soon followed suit. In the meanwhile, the dowries that the sisters brought to the convent provided the financial security necessary to run their various institutions. The increase in the number of convents in Ulster indicated that money was not an obstacle to expansion.

In the 1840s the only convent founded in Ulster was a house of the Poor Clares at Newry, in the diocese of Dromore. In the following decade ten new convents were established. Throughout Ireland the years 1860 to 1870 were called 'the missionary decade' because of the substantial increase in the number of houses. In the north the usual increase in the number of convents was seven in ten years, and in the missionary decade the increase was fifteen.

As well as the expansion of religious houses, there emerged a geographical distribution from east to west. The majority of convents were founded in the eastern dioceses of Down and Connor, and Armagh. This trend reflected the prosperous commercial and industrial condition of the east coast, centred on the port and city of Belfast, where the Catholic middle classes had been established. The wealth generated in this region meant that its inhabitants could afford to support a religious community.

In the 1860s the Mercy congregations ran nine of the fifteen new convents established in Ulster.

Catherine McAuley, a rich Dublin woman, established a community of women who shared their belongings, took private vows and carried out various charitable activities. In 1828 they were granted diocesan approval as a secular institute. The independence that these women enjoyed caused some disapproval in hierarchical quarters. McAuley was persuaded to style her community as a religious congregation. The rule of the order was adopted in 1840. Connections with Rome offered the community permanence.

Often several Mercy convents were founded in one diocese in the same year. In Down and Connor convents were opened at Blackmore, Belfast and Downpatrick in 1866. Kilmore, Belturbet and Ballyjamesduff convents date from 1869. Dromore, Rostrevor and Lurgan gained new convents in 1867, while Warrenpoint and Kilmore Street, Newry, opened in 1889.

Once a convent had been established in a diocese, others were able to form more quickly; this is most marked with the Sisters of St Louis, who set up four or five houses in Clogher diocese between 1859 and 1904. Their Middletown convent was established in Armagh diocese. Within three years of each other two of the Poor Clares convents were set up in Kilmore diocese in Cavan (1865) and Ballyjamesduff (1868). Two of the Nazareth convents were in Down and Connor. Ballynafeigh and Ravenhill Road were both in Belfast. Between 1900 and 1913 all of the Holy Cross and Passion convents were established in the diocese. The Dominicans had two convents in Down and Connor, and one in Armagh. Both convents of the Presentation Sisters were in Armagh.

Another trend relating to the spread of convents in the north concerns the primacy of two dioceses, Down and Connor, and Armagh. These were two of the most prosperous dioceses. Belfast was at the centre of an industrial district dominated by linen mills and shipbuilding, and Belfast's economic importance helps to explain the number of convents around it. In 1840 there were no convents in Belfast, but by 1880 there were seven and by 1920 this figure had reached eleven. Armagh had a prosperous agricultural base and of course was the spiritual centre of Ireland and archdiocese of the Catholic Church. Five out of the six orders with only one convent in the north were located in either Down and Connor, or Armagh. Most houses with multiple convents had at least one congregation in each of these dioceses. Out of the total of seventeen orders, only the Marist and Loreto orders did not establish in the two primary dioceses; but these account for only three out of the sixty-two convents that were established in Ulster between 1840 and 1920. Convent locations reinforce the religious importance of Armagh and Belfast in Catholic missionary work.

Ulster convents were involved in the diversity of social activity that also characterised their southern counterparts. In the convents there was an emphasis on education, and over two-thirds of the convents were connected with schools in some form. As early as 1860, 84 per cent of convents in Ireland were involved in schools. Only five out of seventeen orders in Ulster were not involved in education – Nazareth, Good Shepherd, Marist, Mary Immaculate and Bon Secours. These orders were more concerned with social welfare. They ran orphanages and laundries, and were involved with prison-visiting. Altogether they made up for eight of the sixty-two convents, or less than 10 per cent.

Cities attracted social-welfare-oriented and teaching orders. For example, at Belfast, the Mercy convent on Crumlin Road, the Dominicans, Sisters of the Most Holy Cross and Passion, and the Daughters of Charity of St Vincent de Paul all provided educational establishments. The Good Shepherd Convent, Blackmore, Belfast, provided a 'Magdalene Penitentiary'. Women admitted to this convent were often young and pregnant, and accounts of some of these women make this place sound more like a prison than a home for young women. The Mercy convent, Crumlin Road, also provided a reformatory and laundry for a short time. The Mercy convent, Sussex Place, Belfast, ran the Mater Hospital. One of the Nazareth convents provided an old people's home at Blackmore, and one report said that it was the home of old and infirm men and women of all religions. The Sisters of Bon Secours, Alfred Street, Belfast, claimed to attend to the sick of all denominations. Another Nazareth convent was set up in 1917 – only the second one run by nuns in the Down and Connor diocese. The Sisters of Mercy established an orphanage in Belfast by 1865.

Belfast was well looked after in regard to education and social welfare, but smaller towns were fortunate if they housed even one teaching congregation. In Down and Connor eleven convents were concerned with education.

By 1920 the Armagh diocese had seen the establishment of fourteen convents, twelve of which were concerned with teaching. The French Daughters of Charity, Drogheda, and the Poor Clares of Keady, together with the Daughters of Charity of St Vincent de Paul, Drogheda, the Presentation convent, Portadown, and the Mercy convent of Cookstown all provided night schools for working women. These five, in addition to four in Down and Connor and one at Derry, accounted for half of the night schools run by nuns in Ulster at this time. They were all centred in areas of large population, where working women could be found. The night schools at Down and Connor were all concentrated in Belfast, where many women worked in mills and were keen on the idea of night schools. The Daughters of Charity of St Vincent de Paul, in the Armagh diocese, also ran industrial schools at Drogheda.

The only orphanage of the diocese was the St Louis convent at Middletown, where the nuns also had a boarding school and a poor school.

Only the Sisters of Mercy at Ardee were involved in nursing. This house was set up originally in 1865, when three sisters took charge of the local workhouse hospital. Again the emphasis was on education, and the wealth of the diocese is also shown by the lack of nuns working in the workhouse or in the female reformatories.

Apart from Down and Connor, and Armagh, the other dioceses in Ulster suffered from a variety of disadvantages. This made the widespread foundation of convents more difficult. In 1856 one Loreto convent was founded, and in 1867 a Mercy house was set up. The explanation for this seems to be that the diocese lacked modern communications. It had very little commerce or industry and was remote from the centres of industrialisation on the east coast, so it was unable to keep an extensive network of convents. For the convents that were established, their activities reflect the poverty of the area. The Mercy convents at Ballyshannon operated a large poor school, orphanage and workhouse hospital in 1893. Branch houses at Stranorlar and Glenties were unable to sustain independent status until after 1920, and they were connected with the workhouses and in Donegal town to a National poor school.

By 1865 the institute of Loreto at Letterkenny for the education of upper- and middle-class women was announced. This provided a select day school with boarding facilities. The sisters also had a poor school, but the main emphasis was on the select school.

Derry diocese was remote from the prosperity of the east of Ulster, but by 1920 eight convents had been established. Four of the houses were in the city of Londonderry and were attracted by a combination of factors, including a thriving shirt industry, the seaport and the large Catholic population. As in Belfast, about half of the convents were concerned with social welfare and half with education. The two Mercy convents operated a select school, two free schools, and a night school for the women of the shirt factories. The Nazareth Sisters from 1893 controlled an orphanage. The Good Shepherd sisters managed a laundry and female reformatory – one of only four in the whole of Ulster. Londonderry's needs were well catered for in comparison to more rural areas. The other convents of the diocese, such as the Loreto convent, Omagh, and the Mercy convent, Strabane, emphasised the need for schools for young females. The Strabane school educated 130 boarders as well as operating a large free school. The sisters also ran a female orphanage and an industrial school from 1879 onwards. Mercy convents accounted for five out of eight convents in the Derry diocese, reflecting their willingness to work in poor rural regions, populated by small farmers and artisans. In these regions there were pioneers in education for the local Catholic population.

Despite the majority population of Catholics in the west of Ulster, convents were mainly found in the diocese in the north-east; such was the case of the dioceses of Clogher and Kilmore, where the majority of convents were established in two towns close to the east coast. At Clogher six of the eight convents were involved in primary education. From 1858, the Sisters of Mercy ran an industrial school at Enniskillen, bringing the word to hundreds of female children.

Clogher convents combined their education duties with practical work. At the St Louis convent, Monaghan, as well as running a school, they managed one of the four reformatories in Ulster. The Sisters of Mercy at Castleblayney, as well as running a poor school, visited the local prisons and sick poor. Other convents focused on social issues. The Sisters of Mercy ran all three of the convent-managed workhouses in Ulster, one of which was set up in 1905 at Ballyshannon, and here the sisters dealt with destitute families of old people, relying on larger and richer centres of Catholic population to help them financially. At Clogher there were no convents concerned with night schools, orphanages, hospitals, or homes for the old.

Kilmore was a diocese located in the poorer midlands of Ulster, isolated from the industrial north-east. Like Clogher, its six convents were gathered together in the east of the diocese. These included four Mercy convents and two Poor Clares convents. The low level of educational and social-welfare efforts in the diocese was a pointer to the general poverty of the Catholic population. There were no boarding schools or select schools in the district. The Poor Clares were able to sustain poor schools as at Ballyjamesduff and Cavan, although in Cavan they did not run an industrial school as well. This was in contrast to the Dromore diocese, for it was half its size and was able to run six convents, five of which concentrated exclusively on education.

The Belturbet Sisters of Mercy established a fever hospital in 1869, but it had closed down by 1920, perhaps due to lack of funding.

Looking at the distribution of convents by order, it is possible to see in general that orders engaged in a wide range of activities. Only four of the congregations of sisters ran schools without some sort of social-welfare work – the Dominicans, the Presentation Sisters, the Poor Clares and the Loreto sisters. These accounted for only eleven by 1920. The Loreto sisters only ran poor and boarding schools, while the Presentation Sisters and Dominican Sisters also ran night classes for working women. The sisters visited the sick. The Poor Clares ran industrial schools, as well as boarding and night schools. Most of the congregations did a measure of social work. The Sacre Coeur Sisters, the French Daughters of Charity, the Sisters of the Most Holy Cross and Passion and the Daughters of Charity of St Vincent de Paul were on crusade. Only the Sacre Coeur Sisters supplemented this activity with a poor school and a boarding school. The French Daughters of Charity of St Vincent de Paul, together with the Holy Cross and Passion Sisters, did not run any select or boarding schools, but they ran National Schools, night schools and industrial schools.

The busiest congregations were the Sisters of Mercy and the Sisters of St Louis. They were involved with poor schools and boarding schools as well as orphanages and reformatories, and they visited the sick. The Sisters of Mercy were a more dynamic order than the others in terms of organising work. There were seventeen orders in Ulster, but only five were involved in educational work: the Good Shepherd Sisters, who ran the reformatories; the Sisters of Bon Secours, who visited the sick and old; the Nazareth Sisters, who worked in orphanages and old people's homes; the Marist Sisters; and the Mary Immaculate Sisters.

In conclusion, over the course of the nineteenth century the number of convents increased in the province, with the years 1860–70 standing out as the most successful. The trend was towards a concentration of houses around the eastern side of Ulster, where the industries of Belfast gave rise to a prosperous middle class, willing to finance educational and welfare groups. Convents encouraged their members to work as professionals, and women played a key role in their activities. The convent was a haven as well as a place of religious worship. At this time the Catholic Church was a growing body in Ireland and in Europe. Convents provided women with a good deal of work. The spread of convents coincided with a period when other opportunities for female work were becoming more restrictive.

Health care was a paramount concern of the convents in Ulster, as well as social welfare and education for ordinary people. The great success of the Sisters of Mercy is most outstanding. But the years after partition created a set of entirely new challenges for the religious women of Ulster. The study of nuns in Ulster merits considerably more research.

Select Bibliography

Brian Walker: *Past and Present* (Institute of Irish Studies, 2000).

Earl Storey: *Traditional Roots* (The Columba Press, 2002).

Edward Pearce: *Lines of Most Resistance* (Little Brown & Co., 1999).

Janice Holmes and Diane Urquhart (editors): *Coming into the Light* (Institute of Irish Studies, 1994).

John Davis: *Rural Change in Ireland* (Institute of Irish Studies, 1999).

John Stevenson: *Two Centuries of Life in Down, 1600–1800* (The White Row Press, 1990).

Kenneth O. Morgan (editor): *The Young Oxford History of Britain and Ireland* (Oxford University Press, 1996).

Marianne Elliott: *The Catholics of Ulster* (Penguin Books, 2000).

Paul Johnson: *Ireland: A Concise History* (Granada Publishing, 1981).

R. F. Foster: *The Oxford History of Ireland* (Penguin Books, 1989).

R. H. McIlrath: *Early Victorian Larne* (Braid Books, 1991).

Sheelagh Drudy and Kathleen Lynch: *Schools and Society in Ireland* (Gill & Macmillan, 1993).

Simon Lee (editor): *Freedom from Fear* (Institute of Irish Studies, 1990).